More

Sharing the Easter Story

'Imbued with biblical insight, this book delves into the basic human nature of our lives, the failings, the forgivings and the foibles of the way we are and the way we behave. Into the glorious muddle of our lives, we search for God and find God, revealed distinctively in the Easter story. We find God on a journey through repentance and restitution, forgiveness and faith, arriving at the Easter dawn with a renewed sense of our place in the world and the way in which we can and should relate to each other and to God. In Sally Welch we have a delightful, experienced pastoral guide who looks back at lockdowns and opens up new pastures of faith, hope and love as we journey on.'
Gordon Giles, canon chancellor, Rochester Cathedral and author of *At Home in Lent*

'Sally has a wonderful gift of bringing the biblical text alive by connecting its stories and images to contemporary examples we are familiar with and perhaps experience ourselves. The result is fresh insight into God's great overarching story and an invitation to participate in it ourselves.'
Elizabeth Hoare, director of spiritual formation and pastoral care, Wycliffe Hall

'In this both challenging and encouraging Lent book, Sally has woven a beautiful golden cord, binding together scriptural truth and wisdom, profound contemporary relevance and insightful personal experience. Written with warmth, love and understanding, this is a genuine treasure to accompany your Lenten journey and, indeed, for any time or season.'
Margaret Silf, author of *Lighted Windows*

15 The Chambers, Vineyard
Abingdon OX14 3FE
brf.org.uk

Bible Reading Fellowship (BRF) is a charity (233280)
and company limited by guarantee (301324),
registered in England and Wales

ISBN 978 1 80039 098 0
First published 2021
10 9 8 7 6 5 4 3 2 1 0

Acknowledgements
Unless otherwise stated, scripture quotations are taken from The New Revised Standard Version of the Bible, Anglicised Edition, copyright © 1989, 1995 by the Division of Christian Education of the National Council of the Churches of Christ in the USA. Used by permission. All rights reserved. Scripture quotations marked with the following abbreviations are taken from the version shown. NIV: The Holy Bible, New International Version (Anglicised edition) copyright © 1979, 1984, 2011 by Biblica. Used by permission of Hodder & Stoughton Publishers, an Hachette UK company. All rights reserved. 'NIV' is a registered trademark of Biblica. UK trademark number 1448790. GNT: The Good News Bible published by The Bible Societies/HarperCollins Publishers Ltd, UK © American Bible Society 1966, 1971, 1976, 1992, used with permission. NKJV: the New King James Version®. Copyright © 1982 by Thomas Nelson. Used by permission. All rights reserved. KJV: the Authorised Version of the Bible (The King James Bible), the rights in which are vested in the Crown, are reproduced by permission of the Crown's Patentee, Cambridge University Press. NLT: The Holy Bible, New Living Translation, copyright © 1996, 2004, 2007, 2013. Used by permission of Tyndale House Publishers, Inc., Carol Stream, Illinois 60188. All rights reserved. CEV: The Contemporary English Version. New Testament © American Bible Society 1991, 1992, 1995. Old Testament © American Bible Society 1995. Anglicisations © British & Foreign Bible Society 1996. Used by permission. RSV: The Revised Standard Version of the Bible, copyright © 1946, 1952, 1971 by the Division of Christian Education of the National Council of the Churches of Christ in the United States of America. Used by permission. All rights reserved.

A catalogue record for this book is available from the British Library

Printed and bound by CPI Group (UK) Ltd, Croydon CR0 4YY

SHARING THE EASTER STORY

From reading to living the gospel

Sally Welch

To my brother Richard, with heartfelt thanks

Contents

Introduction

One hundred years ago, in 1922, at a church in south London, the Fellowship of St Matthew was begun in response to a congregation's eagerness for informed and helpful support in building a habit of daily Bible reading. In 1926, it became known as the Bible Reading Fellowship (BRF) as its influence spread and more and more church communities subscribed to the notes and prayers which were offered.

Today, BRF resources people and groups as they grow in faith, encouraging them to deepen their relationship with God and to share the good news of Jesus Christ with others.

This Lent study book is written in response to BRF's vision of 'Sharing the Story', by looking at the events leading up to Easter. It will take you on a journey through familiar and unfamiliar parts of the Bible, reading and reflecting on our Christian faith.

But first we need to explore what it means to share our story. For me, it begins with *listening* – listening deeply and carefully, to God, to others, to the world and to ourselves. With careful listening will come a greater degree of *understanding*. We will never understand everything, but as we stretch our minds and our hearts, we will progress and grow – and our faith will deepen also.

Once we have listened to the word of God and understood it as far as we are able, we must take time to *reflect* upon it. During difficult and stressful times, I have found it extremely helpful to take a Bible passage and just spend time thinking about what it means. Sometimes the passage brings wisdom for my situation; sometimes it doesn't speak to that at all, but I gain some other insight.

The process of listening, understanding and reflecting leads to our being able to absorb the passage into our hearts. We begin to *live* the biblical wisdom as we seek to act upon its teaching and adjust our lives accordingly. That is the stage at which we might begin to share with others the insights we have gained, when we begin to *tell* others the story of God's saving love for each of us. Once we have told it, the story is *shared* – we become part of a community of storytellers, of good-news givers, of children of the gospel. Then we may *become* the story we reflect upon, live and share.

And what is this story? What are the elements of the last few weeks of Jesus' life, his death and his resurrection which bring hope to the world? We begin by beginning again – by acknowledging our wrong-doing and seeking God's help to turn our lives around to face the direction in which God is moving. Once we have repented, we can forgive and be forgiven, a constantly renewing challenge to give and receive forgiveness. This is achieved because we place our hope in the resurrection – we witness the kingdom breaking through into our lives and the lives of others, and so reinforce our trust in God and in his Son, who will deliver and redeem all those who put their trust in him. We reflect on the sacrifice of God in Christ and learn what it is to live sacrificial lives ourselves, offering prayer and praise through worship and service to the one who gives us grace without asking for anything in return. As we approach the end of Lent and arrive at the glory of Easter, we can journey boldly wherever God leads us, secure in his love and, through that love, able to love ourselves and to offer love to others, putting our faith in the hope of the kingdom and becoming transformed into God's new creations.

You will notice that all the chapter headings use the present participle – they are all active, 'doing' words. This is because the process is a constant one, full of energy and motion. It is my hope that the Bible stories will take a grip on your imagination, encouraging you to think deeply about all they contain. This book does not aim to prescribe, but to invite you to join me on a journey through Lent to Easter, discovering what it means to 'share the story' of our faith.

Sharing the Easter story as an individual

Every week in Lent you will be introduced to a different element of the Easter story, journeying through the story-sharing process. A short Bible passage is followed by a reflection, a prayer and some questions to help you reflect for yourself on the passage.

You might like to read the passage out loud, slowly and carefully, allowing time to let the words sink in, pausing at the end of each sentence. You might take one sentence or word which stands out for you and learn it by heart, holding it in your thoughts throughout the day, perhaps journalling what it has come to mean for you by the evening.

At the end of each week there is a suggestion for a creative prayer and further questions, which can be used by both groups and individuals.

Sharing the Easter story as a group

The readings and reflections in this book have been set out so that a rhythm of daily study and prayer can be established. In this way a habit of daily encounter with God, which will build us up in our faith and encourage us on our journey, can be formed, renewed or reinforced. I have also tried to encourage the habit of theological reflection by including questions to think about at the end of each day's reflection. These questions can be used by individuals, but also as a group to reflect on the theme of the week.

The suggested timetable is for meetings to take place during the week after the date of the readings in question, and the questions are therefore arranged so that groups can begin during the week after Ash Wednesday (that is, the week commencing Monday 7 March), looking at the material for Week 1 (2–6 March). The final group meeting is after Easter Sunday and can be held that week or the following week. In this way, we can be encouraged to think about what comes next – the story didn't end at Easter!

The readings and reflections in this book can be used in different ways by all sorts of groups. They can form the basis for a weekly Lent group or provide topics of discussion at Lent lunches or suppers. They can be used as conversation-starters for groups that already meet, such as midweek fellowship groups, Mothers' Union meetings or men's breakfasts.

If a new group is beginning and is meeting in person, it is a good idea to include refreshments with each meeting – some groups find an evening meal with discussion round the table very popular, while others feel that drinks and biscuits or cake are more appropriate. This kind of hospitality can break down barriers and introduce people to each other in a relaxed way, which in turn will lead to a livelier, more fruitful discussion.

If you are leading or joining a group, remember that everyone will need their own copy of the book well before the beginning of Lent.

Suggestions for group meetings

The group leader may or may not also be the group host. Either or both of these roles may be fixed for the whole of Lent or rotate among the group.

If the group leader and host are different people, they should liaise beforehand to ensure arrangements are in place, the time and date are fixed and refreshments are available.

Introduction

Make sure each person has a copy of the book and that spares are available for those who do not. Introduce newcomers to the group and make them feel welcome. Remind everyone that they do not have to contribute to the discussion if they don't want to, but that conversation will be livelier if they do!

Opening prayer

Use a prayer within the traditions of the group; this will help put people at ease, and those who are familiar with the traditions will lend confidence to those who are not. A song or hymn can be sung.

Discussion

If the group is large, split into twos or threes to discuss reactions to the week's reflections. Allow time for each person to share, if they wish. If discussion is slow to start, suggest that each person offers one word or sentence that sums up their reaction.

Forum

As one group, try to discern some themes that are common to most people. If it helps, write these down and circulate them among the group.

Reflection

Study the group questions, and spend some time in silence so that individuals can reflect on the theme personally. Come together to discuss the questions. Again, if the group is large, it is helpful to split into smaller groups.

Plenary

The leader draws together the themes arising from the discussion and sees whether they mirror those from the week's reflections. Again, these can be noted for later distribution.

Prayer

It can be helpful to begin your prayer time with silence, in order to meditate on the results of the discussion. Suggestions for creative prayer can be found at the end of every week – these can be used in a group or as an individual. This can be followed by open prayer. Be flexible, allowing time for each person to contribute if they wish.

Closing prayer

Week 1 | Wednesday 2 March–Sunday 6 March

Repenting

We begin our study on Ash Wednesday, that day in the church calendar dedicated to a wholehearted acknowledgement of our sins. Some church traditions sign foreheads with the burnt ashes of last year's palm crosses – a visible, external sign of a repentant soul. This action heralds the start of Lent, a time for reflecting on our lives, attempting to correct the errors that we discover and determining to move forward in God's grace.

Repentance is a complex concept. It begins with that vital first step of recognising our sinfulness – that which we commemorate on Ash Wednesday – but this is only the first step along a lifelong journey of learning to live and love in and through Christ.

Repentance involves accepting and acknowledging our wrongdoing – to ourselves and also to others. Repentance has to be taken into our hearts rather than just spoken on our lips; it must be lived, not just stated.

Repentance involves restitution – we must endeavour to restore that which our actions have damaged and those whom our words have wounded. Where restitution is not possible, we must accept the consequences of our wrongdoing and bear those burdens gracefully and prayerfully.

We must acknowledge that judgement of others is not ours to give and that sharing repentance involves living forgiven lives ourselves rather than telling others how to live. We must take up the offer of the indwelling of the Holy Spirit, made to us at our baptism and constantly renewed each time we ask in penitence and faith.

Finally and most importantly of all, we will see throughout this week that, as well as accepting our wrongdoing, repentance involves accepting our forgiveness as well. Every one of us is an heir to the kingdom. All we must do to inherit it is to ask.

> Those who heard this asked, 'Who then can be saved?' Jesus replied, 'What is impossible with man is possible with God.'
> LUKE 18:26–27 (NIV)

Wednesday 2 March (Ash Wednesday)

Listening, understanding and reflecting

2 Samuel 12:1–15

And the Lord sent Nathan to David. He came to him, and said to him, 'There were two men in a certain city, the one rich and the other poor. The rich man had very many flocks and herds; but the poor man had nothing but one little ewe lamb, which he had bought. He brought it up, and it grew up with him and with his children; it used to eat of his meagre fare, and drink from his cup, and lie in his bosom, and it was like a daughter to him. Now there came a traveller to the rich man, and he was loath to take one of his own flock or herd to prepare for the wayfarer who had come to him, but he took the poor man's lamb, and prepared that for the guest who had come to him.' Then David's anger was greatly kindled against the man. He said to Nathan, 'As the Lord lives, the man who has done this deserves to die; he shall restore the lamb fourfold, because he did this thing, and because he had no pity.'

Nathan said to David, 'You are the man! Thus says the Lord, the God of Israel: I anointed you king over Israel, and I rescued you from the hand of Saul; I gave you your master's house, and your master's wives into your bosom, and gave you the house of Israel and of Judah; and if that had been too little, I would have added as much more. Why have you despised the word of the Lord, to do what is evil in his sight? You have struck down Uriah the Hittite with the sword, and have taken his wife to be your wife, and have killed him with the sword of the Ammonites. Now therefore the sword shall never depart from

your house, for you have despised me, and have taken the wife of Uriah the Hittite to be your wife. Thus says the Lord: I will raise up trouble against you from within your own house; and I will take your wives before your eyes, and give them to your neighbour, and he shall lie with your wives in the sight of this very sun. For you did it secretly; but I will do this thing before all Israel, and before the sun.' David said to Nathan, 'I have sinned against the Lord.' Nathan said to David, 'Now the Lord has put away your sin; you shall not die. Nevertheless, because by this deed you have utterly scorned the Lord, the child that is born to you shall die.' Then Nathan went to his house.

Reflection

Whistle-blowers have a curious reputation in this country. The British government is clear about what constitutes whistle-blowing: 'You're a whistleblower if you're a worker and you report certain types of wrongdoing.' It is also clear that the wrongdoing must be 'in the public interest' and that whistle-blowers are protected by law (see **gov.uk/whistleblowing**).

But the reality is more complicated than that – there is often a feeling that the whistle-blower is somehow at fault: maybe they misinterpreted what was happening or they are being disloyal to their employers. Many times the whistle-blower, although not able to be sacked, leaves their post anyway because they are made to feel so uncomfortable. There is no doubt that whistle-blowing takes courage and determination.

The first character we meet in this story is one of the original whistle-blowers – he is calling out the actions of his king because they are so wrong that they must not continue any longer. Nathan has been sent by God, so he has that degree of certainty on his side, but all the same it must have taken a huge amount of courage to enter the king's chamber and pronounce judgement against the most powerful man in the country. But there is no shirking of his responsibility – as a prophet, Nathan knows that it is his role to hold people to account, to remind them of their obligation to God and to their fellow citizens.

Fortunately for him, Nathan has also been gifted with intelligence and cunning – instead of marching in front of David and baldly listing out David's wrongdoings, he wraps his message within a story. In this way, he hopes to draw David in unawares, encouraging him to think in the abstract about the rights or wrongs of his action, rather than be put immediately on the defensive.

We don't know how David listens to the story – is his imagination immediately captured so that for him the characters become real and he is passionate in his denunciation of them? Or has the enormous power he now wields so corrupted him that he sits back in apathy, pronouncing the death sentence as just one among many careless sentences he passes as king and judge? Either way, the thunderous statement 'You are the man!' must have hit him like a lightning bolt, as David realises he has sat in judgement upon his own actions – and condemned them.

Dear, lovely, flawed David! We prefer our action heroes to be continually brave, continually self-sacrificing, always walking the righteous path. But here the Bible shows us once again how power and wealth can corrupt even the brightest and best of us. Gone is the humble shepherd boy, placing his faith in God and a slingshot. Gone is the beleaguered warrior, hiding in caves from the wrath of a mad king. Here instead is an entitled, despotic ruler, abusing his power and taking whatever he wants.

Those who like their heroes to be untarnished have tried to place the blame on Bathsheba, saying that she tempted David with a glimpse of her naked body, or to opt for the 'true love should let nothing stand in its path' argument to defend David's actions. These are poor reasons indeed for the slaughter of a fellow human being. And when finally

David is forced to confront his own wrongdoing, that original David, buried beneath so much gold and pomp, is revealed once more. In a return to his former brave, trusting self, he doesn't offer any defence or justification: 'I have sinned against the Lord,' he states, admitting his offence and repenting of it in the same breath.

David is forgiven. But all sins have consequences. Although his repentance is genuine and accepted as such, the result of his sin remains – Uriah is still dead, Bathsheba unlawfully taken. And so, the child must die.

Where does this story take us, living today in our less exalted situation, unlikely to have become corrupted by too much power or indeed to have killed another human being? It reminds us that we need courage to confront the wrongdoing in this world, but that nonetheless we must continue to do so. But it also warns us that none of us are sin-free. 'I am that man', we should perhaps be saying to ourselves on a daily basis, calling us to repentance, reminding us that we must first take the log from our own eyes so that we can see clearly to remove the speck from those of our neighbour (Matthew 7:5).

We should not despair, however, nor fall into that mire of self-hatred for all our sins. Our sins will be forgiven – Jesus has died to make this so. And today, Ash Wednesday, is the first step along the road to repentance and forgiveness, as we not only admit our wrongdoing, but also vow to make every effort to put things right and to 'sin no more'. The death of that innocent infant at the end of the story reminds us that sins have consequences which must be lived with even after forgiveness is obtained – these we must put right if we can; endure if we cannot.

Questions

- Think of an occasion when you have witnessed wrongdoing – whether in your personal or work life. How did you react? What was the effect of your actions? On reflection, would you act in the same way again?

- 'You are the man!' What impact does that statement have for you?

Prayer

Loving Father, like David I try to ignore the things I have done wrong. I try to justify my actions; I blame others for my offences; I plead temptation impossible to resist. Help me to face up to my sins and accept responsibility for the many ways in which I have hurt you and others. Lead me towards true repentance and, even though I don't quite achieve this, forgive me anyway. All this for the sake of your Son, Jesus Christ, my Saviour. Amen

Thursday 3 March

Living

Matthew 3:1–11

In those days John the Baptist appeared in the wilderness of Judea, proclaiming, 'Repent, for the kingdom of heaven has come near.' This is the one of whom the prophet Isaiah spoke when he said,

'The voice of one crying out in the wilderness:
"Prepare the way of the Lord,
make his paths straight."'

Now John wore clothing of camel's hair with a leather belt around his waist, and his food was locusts and wild honey. Then the people of Jerusalem and all Judea were going out to him, and all the region along the Jordan, and they were baptised by him in the river Jordan, confessing their sins.

But when he saw many Pharisees and Sadducees coming for baptism, he said to them, 'You brood of vipers! Who warned you to flee from the wrath to come? Bear fruit worthy of repentance. Do not presume to say to yourselves, "We have Abraham as our ancestor"; for I tell you, God is able from these stones to raise up children to Abraham. Even now the axe is lying at the root of the trees; every tree therefore that does not bear good fruit is cut down and thrown into the fire.

'I baptise you with water for repentance, but one who is more powerful than I is coming after me; I am not worthy to carry his sandals. He will baptise you with the Holy Spirit and fire.'

Reflection

We finished our study of repentance yesterday at that moment of extreme crisis and recognition: 'You are the man!' declared Nathan; 'I have sinned against the Lord,' replied David. Fantastic stuff, yes, but just the beginning of the journey of repentance, which is not only lifelong but daily.

It seems from today's reading that simply asking for forgiveness is not enough. The Pharisees and Sadducees who come to John for baptism are told in no small way that John's baptism is not the end of it – they must truly live their repentance. The leaders of the Jewish religious authorities thought they had it all sorted – they kept the laws, they were diligent in prayer and in attending worship at the temple. It was all under control. But John looked into their hearts and saw pride, selfishness, arrogance and hypocrisy, and he called them out. It isn't enough to follow the law with your heads, he says to them; you must live it in your hearts.

Today is a good time to ponder whether we, too, aren't a bit guilty of behaving like the Pharisees and Sadducees. When we gather in church or reflect privately and consider our sins, are we really conscious of having 'trespassed' against God and against our neighbour? Or do we secretly feel that our sins are not such great ones – or, at least, not as great as those of other people we know – and maybe we don't need to repent quite so heartily. This process of allowing our repentance to move from being on our lips to in our hearts happens gradually and constantly, and must be continually refreshed, as we remind ourselves again and again of how short we fall of all that we can be and do.

The daughter of a friend of mine has a young child, and although she delights in being a mother and dotes on her son, she occasionally struggles with 'parental guilt'. She wants desperately to be the best parent she can be, but is aware that she falls short time and again – when her tiredness makes her impatient; when reading the same book for the 15th time is not enjoyable; when the prospect of another rainy afternoon playing cars in the living room fills her with boredom rather than excitement. Raising a child is a humbling business!

But lived repentance is not about feeling guilty all the time – that would be tiring and fruitless. The origin of the word 'repent', we are frequently told, includes the concept of turning away from old habits and attitudes and turning towards a new way of life. Repentance is an action, not just a thought. It requires positive choice, a determination to move forward in a new way, reclaiming our humanity and putting it to the service of God and others.

That new mother is learning to accept perfect parenting doesn't exist – but heartfelt parenting does, and it is the better option. Perfect repentance would mean a perfect life. As human beings, that is beyond our ability. But each day offers fresh opportunities for new beginnings, better choices and positive steps along the road of the kingdom.

A repentant life is a joyful one. It is an 'I can' experience: I can change; I can grow; I can live more fully. But it is also an 'I can't experience': I can't do this alone. Only from God will we find true repentance; only through Christ can we be wholly forgiven; only with the Spirit can we live out that repentance, bearing fruit worthy of that constant renewing of our hearts and minds, turning again and again towards the light which shows us the way.

And there is one further step – that of restitution. As part of repentance, we should seek to put right that which we have made wrong. Thus Jesus instructs us to seek reconciliation with those with whom we have argued before coming to worship:

> If you are offering your gift at the altar and there remember that your brother or sister has something against you, leave your gift there in front of the altar. First go and be reconciled to them; then come and offer your gift.
> MATTHEW 5:23–24 (NIV)

Sadly this may not always be possible – those whom we have wronged may not accept our apology; the damage caused by our actions might be irreversible; it may be too late to put things right. Then we must bear this as best we can – the life of David's child was not spared and David had to accept the consequences of his sin, striving only not to make the same mistake in the future.

Questions

- What relationship can you improve or change? Perhaps one needs to be ended before it damages you further.
- Think of one way in which you could improve your use of time. This could be significant, such as taking up a Bible study, joining a prayer group or serving in church, or not so dramatic, such as trying to pray every time you put the kettle on or getting up earlier to make some time in your day to reflect.
- Think of one habit or activity you would like to take up – or put down. Be imaginative and creative in your thinking; it doesn't just have to be about running or smoking!

Prayer

Help me, dear Lord, to bear fruits worthy of repentance. Show me a picture of a repentant life and draw me ever closer to your heart. Amen

Friday 4 March

Telling

Acts 2:36–42

'Therefore let the entire house of Israel know with certainty that God has made him both Lord and Messiah, this Jesus whom you crucified.'

Now when they heard this, they were cut to the heart and said to Peter and to the other apostles, 'Brothers, what should we do?' Peter said to them, 'Repent, and be baptised every one of you in the name of Jesus Christ so that your sins may be forgiven; and you will receive the gift of the Holy Spirit. For the promise is for you, for your children, and for all who are far away, everyone whom the Lord our God calls to him.' And he testified with many other arguments and exhorted them, saying, 'Save yourselves from this corrupt generation.' So those who welcomed his message were baptised, and that day about three thousand persons were added. They devoted themselves to the apostles' teaching and fellowship, to the breaking of bread and the prayers.

Reflection

It is easy to tell when a two-year-old is engaged in an activity that they should not be doing. One moment the room is filled with the constant chatter of a small person as they make sense of their world, driving toy cars over the carpet, building brick towers or looking at picture books. They are safe, happy and occupied and we continue with our conversations or our tasks. The next minute, there is silence – the background of babble has ceased and the child has disappeared. Frantic searching reveals that they have discovered the biscuit tin or the china cupboard or have ventured into the study, filled with forbidden mysteries. Then comes the conversation – no, you can't eat all the biscuits; no, you can't build castles with china cups; no, you certainly can't play Granny's harp without her being there!

Or perhaps they have been playing happily alongside another child and then suddenly war breaks out over a coveted toy. Hair is pulled, limbs are grabbed and tears follow. Once again we launch into a discussion over the need to be kind to others and to share our toys, even our best ones. As children grow, the conversations become more complex. No longer is it just enough to say no – young people must be given a reason why their behaviour is not acceptable and encouraged to acknowledge that what they have done is wrong. Meaningful apologies must be made, and restitution required.

All this is a vital part of our education. And it is a very challenging one – saying sorry is difficult; admitting guilt makes us feel small and ashamed; making restitution is costly. Taking responsibility for our actions and their consequences is challenging for children and doesn't get much easier for adults, which is why Peter is giving it to the children of Israel with both barrels. Only by expressing clearly and forcibly exactly what they have done in killing Jesus will they be brought to the realisation of their responsibility and, from there, to the act of repentance. 'God has made him both Lord and Messiah, this Jesus whom you crucified,' he bellows, leaving us in no doubt as to the degree of blame and where it lies. And it works – Peter's hearers are 'cut to the heart'. They know that action is required, and they are given directions – 'Repent, and be baptised.'

We have moved one step further in the process of repentance, from first acknowledging sin, then turning from it and now to receiving the gift necessary to live a forgiven life – that of the Holy Spirit. All those who repent and are baptised will receive the Holy Spirit, Peter promises – 'every one of you'. What a fantastic, generous gesture! From the moment of baptism, the Holy Spirit will live within each one of us, enabling us to fulfil God's purposes for us, to live a fully human, forgiven life, taking part in the adventure of the kingdom. God's Messiah is not the end of the story – the story has expanded to take in God's children in relationship with the Messiah and each other by the working of the Holy Spirit. And this relationship will continue to expand, deepen and grow, for its promise extends ever outwards: 'The promise is for you, for your children, and for all.'

Peter spoke, the Spirit moved and the people repented. Now the Spirit can move within the people and God's work on earth will be done. Undoubtedly it could have been achieved without us, but working with us and through us is how God chose to accomplish his will. That in itself is a marvellous affirmation of who we are and what we can achieve in God's name. He trusts us to continue his work, to tell his story.

Because that is where the work begins. The fact of salvation is assured for 'everyone whom the Lord our God calls to him'. But how will they hear him calling? As Paul writes:

> But how are they to call on one in whom they have not believed? And how are they to believe in one of whom they have never heard? And how are they to hear without someone to proclaim him?
>
> ROMANS 10:14

It is important not to confuse telling people about repentance with ordering people to repent. Peter can do that; I am inclined to think that we cannot. Besides, personal testimony is powerful. Just as leading children through the process of understanding what they have done, why it was wrong and what they can do about that is more effective than simply meting out punishment, so telling others your story and the effect God has had on your life is so much more powerful than simply demanding repentance.

Part of repentance, part of living a new life, part of being in relationship with God is telling others that best of all stories. We should do this; with the help of the Holy Spirit, we can.

Questions

- Spend a few minutes today thinking about your own 'journey of repentance'. It might be one action that you did for which you felt regret and made amends, or it might be a dramatic moment of realisation such as that of the children of Israel whom Peter addresses. What made it so special for you? What inclined you to repentance? Looking back, has your life changed?
- If you were to tell others about this, how would you do so?

Prayer

Almighty God, bestow upon us the meaning of words, the light of understanding, the nobility of diction and the faith of the true nature. And grant that what we believe we may also speak.
St Hilary (315–67)

Saturday 5 March

Sharing

Jonah 3

The word of the Lord came to Jonah a second time, saying, 'Get up, go to Nineveh, that great city, and proclaim to it the message that I tell you.' So Jonah set out and went to Nineveh, according to the word of the Lord. Now Nineveh was an exceedingly large city, a three days' walk across. Jonah began to go into the city, going a day's walk. And he cried out, 'Forty days more, and Nineveh shall be overthrown!' And the people of Nineveh believed God; they proclaimed a fast, and everyone, great and small, put on sackcloth.

When the news reached the king of Nineveh, he rose from his throne, removed his robe, covered himself with sackcloth, and sat in ashes. Then he had a proclamation made in Nineveh: 'By the decree of the king and his nobles: No human being or animal, no herd or flock, shall taste anything. They shall not feed, nor shall they drink water. Human beings and animals shall be covered with sackcloth, and they shall cry mightily to God. All shall turn from their evil ways and from the violence that is in their hands. Who knows? God may relent and change his mind; he may turn from his fierce anger, so that we do not perish.'

When God saw what they did, how they turned from their evil ways, God changed his mind about the calamity that he had said he would bring upon them; and he did not do it.

Reflection

We all know the story of Jonah, don't we? It's one of those vivid, dramatic episodes which can so easily be brought to life – Jonah the reluctant prophet; Jonah the storm-bringer; Jonah the whale-snack. We join the story here as Jonah has learnt that wherever he goes, whether he should 'rise on the wings of the dawn' or 'settle on the far side of the sea' (Psalm 139:9, NIV), he cannot flee from God. More than that, Jonah has discovered that he doesn't want to escape God. He repents of his previous action and, embracing fully the concept of repentance, he travels to Nineveh, to obey God's instructions. But he is still a reluctant prophet. Why is this?

The answer lies in his angry response later in the book, after the people of Nineveh have repented and the city is saved. Jonah is furious that God has not delivered the promised punishment and, he tells God angrily, that is the real reason that he didn't want to prophesy to Nineveh in the first place. He knew this would happen: 'I knew that you are a gracious and compassionate God, slow to anger and abounding in love, a God who relents from sending calamity' (Jonah 4:2, NIV).

Why didn't Jonah want God to deliver the Ninevites? Quite simply because Jonah hated them. He didn't want the people of Nineveh to be saved. Perhaps his vision of heaven did not include consorting with the citizens of that place; perhaps he thought they shouldn't be forgiven because what they had done was too horrible. Far from wanting to bring God's graciousness and compassion to them, he wanted them kept away from repentance and salvation.

There are echoes here of the incident of the Gerasene swine (Mark 5). Once Jesus has healed the man possessed of demons, sending them into the herd of pigs, the people of that place beg Jesus to 'leave their region' (Mark 5:17, NIV). The people don't want to deal with change; they don't want their preconceptions overturned; they don't want to consider their own lives in the light of what has happened. So too with

Jonah – for him the Ninevites are the wicked ones, beyond saving. Bad enough to be sent to that place to preach repentance; worse still for that preaching to take effect!

I occasionally have access to celebrity magazines – in the dentist's waiting room or at the hairdresser's – and it seems to me that most articles fall into one of two groups. One set of stories are full of breathless admiration for a celebrity – their house, their children, their glorious, glamorous lifestyle. These are held up to us as something to envy and to emulate. The other set, however, are the opposite. These chart the fall of people from popularity, the break-up of their relationships, the drop in their income or the rise in their weight. That most pernicious of sins, schadenfreude (the visceral, secret, guilty pleasure we take in the downfall of others), is displayed for all of us to wallow in as we read of the misfortune of others. And it's good to have a scapegoat, isn't it? It's good to have someone with whom we can compare ourselves favourably. However sinful we are, at least we are not as bad as those others.

But that is not how God works. Time and again God demonstrates that with or without us, his will is done. And it is done in Nineveh – despite Jonah, rather than because of him. Despite Jonah delivering one of the worst calls to repentance I have read! Not for Jonah the persuasive arguments of Peter or the inculturation of Paul; no, eight words only are used. It is easy to imagine Jonah strolling through the city crying out, 'Forty days more, and Nineveh shall be overthrown!', secretly hoping that his words will be ignored. But just eight words, and the people repent. Just eight words, and the city of Nineveh is saved.

The message we carry might not be the one we wish to. Too often our own sinfulness makes us unsuitable candidates for highlighting the sins of others. But God will find his own way. It is a truism that human beings cannot 'bring God' to a place or a person, for God is already there.

Questions

- We are all Jonahs. Who are our Ninevites? Who are the people we love to hate?
- Which group or individual might God be calling you to minister to? What are your feelings about this?
- Does your reluctance spring from fear of losing what you have, or losing the certainty that you might not be as righteous as you always believed?

Prayer

God of mercy and grace, forgive me for the times when I have wished ill on others. Forgive my envy, my ignorance, my arrogance, my prejudice. Help me to recognise the face of Christ in those around me; guard me from scapegoating others to make me feel better about myself. As I journey along the road of repentance, may my life be an example and an encouragement to others, not a block. Above all, Father, speak through me; let your words be on my tongue. For I know that with you, nothing is impossible. Amen

| Sunday 6 March

Becoming

Luke 18:18–23; 19:1–10

A certain ruler asked him, 'Good Teacher, what must I do to inherit eternal life?' Jesus said to him, 'Why do you call me good? No one is good but God alone. You know the commandments: "You shall not commit adultery; You shall not murder; You shall not steal; You shall not bear false witness; Honour your father and mother."' He replied, 'I have kept all these since my youth.' When Jesus heard this, he said to him, 'There is still one thing lacking. Sell all that you own and distribute the money to the poor, and you will have treasure in heaven; then come, follow me.' But when he heard this, he became sad; for he was very rich…

[Jesus] entered Jericho and was passing through it. A man was there named Zacchaeus; he was a chief tax-collector and was rich. He was trying to see who Jesus was, but on account of the crowd he could not, because he was short in stature. So he ran ahead and climbed a sycomore tree to see him, because he was going to pass that way. When Jesus came to the place, he looked up and said to him, 'Zacchaeus, hurry and come down; for I must stay at your house today.' So he hurried down and was happy to welcome him. All who saw it began to grumble and said, 'He has gone to be the guest of one who is a sinner.' Zacchaeus stood there and said to the Lord, 'Look, half of my possessions, Lord, I will give to the poor; and if I have defrauded anyone of anything, I will pay back four times as much.' Then Jesus said to him, 'Today salvation has come to this house, because he too is a son of Abraham. For the Son of Man came to seek out and to save the lost.'

Reflection

We see it in all the action movies – the terrified victim, in fear of their lives, leaning out of a burning building, clinging on to a storm-wrecked boat or trapped by a hail of bullets. Then in sweeps the rescuer, swaying at the top of a ladder, swinging from a rope lowered by helicopter or racing forward in an armoured car. 'Jump!' they shout. But the victim hesitates, pausing for one fear-filled moment, afraid to leave certainty, even the certainty of death, for the risk of the unknown. Eventually they do jump, of course, and the film ends happily.

The two men we meet today are both in a desperate position. They both want to be saved, but the story only ends happily for one of them. Ironically it would seem that the man with the best chance comes out worst, as is the way with all good stories.

The rich young man has it all going for him – he is wealthy, is of the right family and lives his life according to the demands of his faith. He approaches Jesus with the confidence of one who is doing everything right. He may even think he already has the answer to his question and is asking it solely as a formality, as reassurance that he is going the right way about achieving that final goal, ticking that one last aspirational box. But Jesus looks at him and sees his inner emptiness, the way he clings on to material possessions and makes a god of them, leaving no room for God within his soul. Jesus offers him a life raft, a ladder out of his pit, but the rich young man cannot bring himself to let go of the objects which prop up his ego, and the opportunity of salvation is rejected.

Our other hero, Zacchaeus, is more of an anti-hero. He is an outcast – he is despised and reviled for his occupation. He has wealth, but he recognises the emptiness of his life. He brings nothing but a desperate desire to see whether Jesus really does have the answer to the question of the meaning of life – why else would he be clinging to a tree, all dignity cast aside, just for a glimpse of the Master? He recognises a rescue when he sees it and as he jumps from the tree, he leaves behind all that he previously clung to.

It is interesting to imagine what Jesus might have said to Zacchaeus once they were in his house together. I suspect he didn't need to say much – just the sheer act of recognising Zacchaeus and spending time with him will have been enough. Jesus probably didn't preach repentance at all; he simply offered Zacchaeus the experience of unconditional love which is to be found in placing one's entire life in God's hands. Having reached out for the life-saving offer, Zacchaeus has found safety and security, so much so that he can let go of his wealth. For in becoming a true child of God, Zacchaeus becomes truly repentant and offers restitution to all those against whom he previously offended: 'Half of my possessions, Lord, I will give to the poor.'

The difference between the rich young man and Zacchaeus is what they ask of Jesus. The rich young man offers Jesus a transactional interpretation of salvation: what do I have to do? He sees the way to eternal life as one of reciprocity – in return for following certain rules, living in a certain way, a certain benefit will be obtained. When Jesus refuses this offer, the man is perplexed and saddened. He lacks the courage to let go of the material versions of 'truth' to which he clings so tightly. He is afraid to reach out and take hold of his rescuer's hand, and his opportunity for redemption is lost, for now. Zacchaeus, however, knows the true value of wealth and material goods. He knows he can offer Jesus nothing except to be open to his call – and he discovers that he is not in fact seeking Jesus so much as Jesus is looking for him! Zacchaeus' question – and ours – is not 'What do I have to do?' but 'Will you come and live in me?' Not doing, but being.

Questions

- What form does your 'sinking ship' take? Do you put your trust in material possessions to bolster you through challenging times? Do you rely too much on the people around you? Do you use food and drink to mask your feelings of sinfulness? How might you move further away from these, and reach out to the saving hand of Jesus? How could you get nearer your 'life raft'?

Prayer

Help me, Father, to acknowledge my sin and to turn away from it. Help me to walk in a new direction, placing my feet in your footsteps, allowing your Holy Spirit to fill my heart and soul so that my words and actions might be your instruments of saving grace. Amen

 Questions for group study

- Reflecting on this week's Bible passages, which ones have engaged you most? Which have you found most challenging? Has your understanding of repentance changed and, if so, how?

- Do you agree that repentance is a process rather than a single action? What steps have you discerned in the Bible passages this week?

- How can we live a repentant life? What is the 'fruit worthy of repentance'? Rather than overwhelming ourselves with all that we might do, perhaps choose three things we wish to change – three things which will put us in a better place with God and with humanity.

Creative prayer

You will need: a mirror; paper towel or tissue.

Look at yourself in the mirror. Breathe on the glass so that the image of yourself is blurred. Look at yourself and say:

> *How can I be saved?*

Pray these words, or others which resonate with your heart:

> *Forgive me, Father, for I have sinned.*

Using the paper towel or tissue, clear away the moisture, saying to your reflection:

> *Remove my sin, and I will be clean;*
> *wash me, and I will be whiter than snow.*
> PSALM 51:7 (GNT)

Then remind yourself that nothing is impossible with God (see Luke 18:26–27).

Finally repeat several times out loud:

> *Take heart… your sins are forgiven.*
> MATTHEW 9:2

Week 2 | Monday 7 March–Sunday 13 March

Forgiving

'Two other men, both criminals, were also led out with [Jesus] to be executed. When they came to the place called the Skull, they crucified him there, along with the criminals – one on his right, the other on his left. Jesus said, "Father, forgive them, for they do not know what they are doing"' (Luke 23:32–34, NIV).

So our Lord and Saviour completes his saving action – by asking for forgiveness on our behalf. Forgiveness – that wonderful, healing and life-transforming gift won for each one of us and presented to us freely and endlessly. But we must make space for this gift, for it will change our attitudes and our lives if we use it properly. We must first clear out our sins by repenting and restoring what we can. Then, having metaphorically swept the house clean, we can allow forgiveness to enter and fill our hearts and souls.

Forgiveness doesn't depend on restitution; it doesn't require that others acknowledge their own sin before we forgive them. That is wonderful when it happens, but it is not a requirement. Forgiveness is not an action; it is a process. Much like its sister, repentance, forgiveness needs to be lived. It needs to be taken up each day and implemented in every word and action. Forgiveness does not involve judgement, only mercy, and a constant awareness that although none of us are worthy, every one of us is invited to the feast.

Monday 7 March

Listening

Genesis 18:17–33

The Lord said, 'Shall I hide from Abraham what I am about to do, seeing that Abraham shall become a great and mighty nation, and all the nations of the earth shall be blessed in him? No, for I have chosen him, that he may charge his children and his household after him to keep the way of the Lord by doing righteousness and justice; so that the Lord may bring about for Abraham what he has promised him.' Then the Lord said, 'How great is the outcry against Sodom and Gomorrah and how very grave their sin! I must go down and see whether they have done altogether according to the outcry that has come to me; and if not, I will know.'

So the men turned from there, and went towards Sodom, while Abraham remained standing before the Lord. Then Abraham came near and said, 'Will you indeed sweep away the righteous with the wicked? Suppose there are fifty righteous within the city; will you then sweep away the place and not forgive it for the fifty righteous who are in it? Far be it from you to do such a thing, to slay the righteous with the wicked, so that the righteous fare as the wicked! Far be that from you! Shall not the Judge of all the earth do what is just?' And the Lord said, 'If I find at Sodom fifty righteous in the city, I will forgive the whole place for their sake.' Abraham answered, 'Let me take it upon myself to speak to the Lord, I who am but dust and ashes. Suppose five of the fifty righteous are lacking? Will you destroy the whole city for lack of five?' And he said, 'I will not destroy it if I find forty-five there.' Again he spoke to him, 'Suppose forty are found there.' He answered, 'For the sake of

forty I will not do it.' Then he said, 'Oh do not let the Lord be angry if I speak. Suppose thirty are found there.' He answered, 'I will not do it, if I find thirty there.' He said, 'Let me take it upon myself to speak to the Lord. Suppose twenty are found there.' He answered, 'For the sake of twenty I will not destroy it.' Then he said, 'Oh do not let the Lord be angry if I speak just once more. Suppose ten are found there.' He answered, 'For the sake of ten I will not destroy it.' And the Lord went his way, when he had finished speaking to Abraham; and Abraham returned to his place.

Reflection

I admit to being a secret fan of both *Bargain Hunt* and *Antiques Road Trip*. For those who have not experienced these television programmes, they are essentially vicarious shopping trips – we watch professionals and amateurs scouring antique shops for things to sell at auction in the hope of making a profit. The fun comes in watching the shoppers bargaining with the experienced stallholders and occasionally triumphing as they purchase for a very low price an object which turns out to be valuable, rare or trendy and thus sells at an exorbitant price. I think I also enjoy the programmes because they show people doing things I never have the nerve to undertake – bargaining with someone to get a lower price. I would rather just pay the ticket price than go through that excruciating process.

I can only have admiration for Abraham, as an initial reading of this passage seems to show Abraham achieving truly amazing results when he bargains successfully – with God! But, as usual, there is more to learn than simply how to beat someone down on price, even when that price is measured in lives.

There is never any doubt that Sodom and Gomorrah are deeply unpleasant cities. All sorts of sinful things are occurring there which can be neither justified nor allowed to continue. And God has plans to sort things out – dramatic and draconian plans. This is one of the rare occasions when we are given an insight into God's thought processes as he muses on whether to share with Abraham his plans for the complete destruction of the two cities. But to act without explanation would be to break the covenant he has entered into with the father of Israel. In the future, Abraham will have to lead his people as they live in 'righteousness and justice', so he needs to be a part of the conversation about the fate of the unrighteous and unjust. In this way God can prepare Abraham for his task of pursuing justice and understanding the consequences. He does this by that best of all teaching methods – engaging Abraham in the decision-making, helping him to understand the reasons behind it and opening the conversation up to becoming a dialogue, not a diatribe. While it appears that God is listening to Abraham, it is in fact Abraham who listens to God, and learns through the process.

To give him his due, Abraham is horrified at the fate that God proposes for Sodom and Gomorrah. But his concern is not for the sinners but for anyone who is still struggling to live a righteous life within the debauched and corrupt cities. Collateral damage – a euphemism which conceals the harshness of the fate of the innocent caught in the crossfire of conflict – is not something that Abraham is prepared to accept. As a prophet, Abraham communicates the mercy of God – those who do not, like Jonah, are soon trained in the right way.

Here Abraham finds himself communicating God's mercy back to him – reminding him that the 'Judge of all the earth' must 'do what is just'. Abraham is aware of his temerity in doing this, but so great is his conviction that he feels he must speak. And God allows himself to be negotiated down from fifty to ten righteous souls being all that is needed to save the city. But just as we suspect that behind-the-scenes negotiations take place in television programmes, so this very negotiation is part of God's plan. Thus Abraham learns of the depths of God's mercy.

And what about us? What do we learn? We learn the power of righteous people. Just as the existence of only ten prayerful citizens could have saved the inhabitants of Sodom, so can we save others today. By our prayers, by our actions and by the witness of our lives we can seek to preserve the world from self-destruction. What a wonderful thought! No longer need we feel powerless because there are so few of us – it only takes a few. As Jesus himself reminds us, we are the salt of the earth, the yeast in the flour (Matthew 5:13; 13:33). There doesn't need to be many of us, because we are enough. God will take our representations, our negotiations on behalf of humanity, and through them will save many. Jesus Christ was sent to save the sinners, not the righteous. The righteous have their own work to do in interceding on behalf of others, asking for forgiveness for the sins of humankind, learning that righteousness and justice will be accomplished.

We also learn that prayer is a conversation, and that this conversation can be started by God as well as by ourselves. So often we launch into our time of prayer with a breathless litany, a rush of all the things that need to be said, explained, sorrowed over, requested. We won't hear what God has to say to us if we don't allow time to listen. We won't hear of his great mercy, the unfathomable depths of forgiveness and redemption which are available to us, unless we are silent before the Lord. Only then will we hear the drop of the 'still dews of quietness', refreshing our souls.

Questions

- Have you ever 'bargained with God'? What did you bargain for? In the light of this passage, what would you bargain for now?
- God's judgement upon Sodom and Gomorrah was fierce and uncompromising – fewer than ten righteous inhabitants were found and thus God destroyed the cities. How does this make you feel about God?
- What would it feel like to know that because of your righteous living, your community would be saved?

Prayer

Drop thy still dews of quietness,
till all our strivings cease.
Take from our souls the strain and stress
until our ordered lives confess
the beauty of thy peace.

John Greenleaf Whittier (1807–92)

Tuesday 8 March

Understanding

Matthew 18:21–35

Then Peter came and said to him, 'Lord, if another member of the church sins against me, how often should I forgive? As many as seven times?' Jesus said to him, 'Not seven times, but, I tell you, seventy-seven times.

'For this reason the kingdom of heaven may be compared to a king who wished to settle accounts with his slaves. When he began the reckoning, one who owed him ten thousand talents was brought to him; and, as he could not pay, his lord ordered him to be sold, together with his wife and children and all his possessions, and payment to be made. So the slave fell on his knees before him, saying, "Have patience with me, and I will pay you everything." And out of pity for him, the lord of that slave released him and forgave him the debt. But that same slave, as he went out, came upon one of his fellow-slaves who owed him a hundred denarii; and seizing him by the throat, he said, "Pay what you owe." Then his fellow-slave fell down and pleaded with him, "Have patience with me, and I will pay you." But he refused; then he went and threw him into prison until he should pay the debt. When his fellow-slaves saw what had happened, they were greatly distressed, and they went and reported to their lord all that had taken place. Then his lord summoned him and said to him, "You wicked slave! I forgave you all that debt because you pleaded with me. Should you not have had mercy on your fellow-slave, as I had mercy on you?" And in anger his lord handed him over to be tortured until he should pay his entire debt. So my heavenly Father will also do to every one of you, if you do not forgive your brother or sister from your heart.'

Reflection

During the various lockdowns and tier-assigning activities of 2020, one of my most soul-destroying tasks was to work out how to apply both the government and the Church of England guidance to my churches. New regulations would arrive with monotonous regularity or, worse still, adjustments to the old regulations – adjustments which were so finely tuned they were almost indiscernible but nevertheless meant a complete revision of the safety notices/risk assessments/service production. It seemed that these regulations would appear on a Friday night, allowing just enough time to rework everything in time for Sunday, but not enough time to do so at a comfortable speed or in a relaxed manner. The wording, too, was open to a wide variety of interpretation, and hours would be spent discussing how a particular set of guidance could be worked out so that the easiest or most satisfying solution was reached. I have a vivid memory of a heated discussion with an archdeacon who accused me (rightly) of adhering to the letter 'but absolutely not the spirit' of one set of guidelines.

I wonder if this was the sort of thing Peter was aiming for when he asked Jesus that loaded question about the number of times he should forgive someone. He might have been looking for a simple, straightforward answer – the kind that makes everything clear-cut, is easy to abide by and has the added advantage of making us feel virtuous for sticking to it.

Because transactional relationships are easier, aren't they? The sort of relationship where it is understood from the outset that one side will deliver one thing and the other side does the same. So, argues Peter, I will allow a certain person to offend against me so many times, then I can consider the entire episode finished with. My obligations to understanding that person, to working for reconciliation and agreement, are at an end the moment that person offends for the final time. Peter shows that he is willing to go the extra mile to forgive someone, as he proposes that an individual might be allowed to hurt him more than once. He is willing to suffer up to seven times before putting an end to the relationship.

But the kingdom of God is not transactional. It does not allow us to make a map of the route to the destination, plotting in numbers of offences forgiven any more than we might chart the numbers of times we have been to church or been kind to our neighbours. Interestingly, in the parable of the unforgiving servant, Jesus not only shows how forgiveness operates, but also demonstrates the brokenness of living an unforgiving life. The servant has constructed a transactional world where mercy counts for nothing. Instead of passing on what he has received, he reverts to the old way and is thus caught up in the darkness of life outside the kingdom. He brings the judgement on himself through his own inflexible systems. I am reminded of Shylock in *The Merchant of Venice*, who, determined to take the pound of flesh allowed him by law from the body of his debtor, Antonio, is in turn subject to a merciless punishment of his own creation.

Forgiveness, says Christ, is not a finite process; it is a way of life. As such, it is a constant, permanent feature of the kingdom. Forgiveness is uncomfortable in that it doesn't require reciprocity – those who have offended against us do not have to first admit they have wronged us before we forgive them. We should not focus on the offence or the offender. It is not even necessary that they are aware we have forgiven them. We may never receive restitution and we may have to live permanently with the damage that has been inflicted upon us, but neither of those affects the obligation we are under as children of God to live forgiving lives. Because before we were ever able to forgive others, we were ourselves forgiven. We were forgiven completely and utterly by virtue of the operation of Christ in his life, death and resurrection. Not only were we forgiven, but we continue to live forgiven lives, and in so doing can reach out to forgive others.

Questions

Ask yourself some hard questions:

- Who do you find it hard to forgive? Why is this?
- How transactional is your method of forgiveness – do you need a quid pro quo?
- What are you waiting for before you forgive?

Prayer

For it is in giving that we receive.
It is in pardoning that we are pardoned.
And it is in dying that we are born to eternal life.
Francis of Assisi (c. 1181–1226)

Wednesday 9 March

Reflecting

Luke 7:36–50

One of the Pharisees asked Jesus to eat with him, and he went into the Pharisee's house and took his place at the table. And a woman in the city, who was a sinner, having learned that he was eating in the Pharisee's house, brought an alabaster jar of ointment. She stood behind him at his feet, weeping, and began to bathe his feet with her tears and to dry them with her hair. Then she continued kissing his feet and anointing them with the ointment. Now when the Pharisee who had invited him saw it, he said to himself, 'If this man were a prophet, he would have known who and what kind of woman this is who is touching him – that she is a sinner.' Jesus spoke up and said to him, 'Simon, I have something to say to you.' 'Teacher,' he replied, 'speak.' 'A certain creditor had two debtors; one owed five hundred denarii, and the other fifty. When they could not pay, he cancelled the debts for both of them. Now which of them will love him more?' Simon answered, 'I suppose the one for whom he cancelled the greater debt.' And Jesus said to him, 'You have judged rightly.' Then turning towards the woman, he said to Simon, 'Do you see this woman? I entered your house; you gave me no water for my feet, but she has bathed my feet with her tears and dried them with her hair. You gave me no kiss, but from the time I came in she has not stopped kissing my feet. You did not anoint my head with oil, but she has anointed my feet with ointment. Therefore, I tell you, her sins, which were many, have been forgiven; hence she has shown great love. But the one to whom little is forgiven, loves little.' Then he said to her, 'Your sins are forgiven.' But

those who were at the table with him began to say among themselves, 'Who is this who even forgives sins?' And he said to the woman, 'Your faith has saved you; go in peace.'

Reflection

> If I ever reach heaven I expect to find three wonders there: first, to meet some I had not thought to see there; second, to miss some I had expected to see there; and third, the greatest wonder of all, to find myself there.
>
> John Newton (1725–1807)

I have just taken a test on the internet designed to find out whether I am destined for heaven or hell. I answered it truthfully and discovered the awful news that I am, in fact, bound for hell. The website then went on to describe in graphic detail all the horrors that await me there and proceeded to tell me the enormities of sin that I should avoid if I were to escape this appalling doom.

It's true: I do deserve to go to hell. I am not good all the time, and I have much to repent of. My chances of not sinning ever again are pretty small, and so, therefore, are my chances of getting to heaven. But that is where this gospel reading comes in.

This gospel reading is vital and fundamental to our way of thinking about Christianity and about the sacrament which we are about to share. It is about forgiveness. It is about being forgiven and forgiving others. Both are easy to say and enormously difficult to do.

This is the first part of the message of today's gospel reading. Jesus is at dinner when he is approached by a woman with a dubious reputation. In those days, formal meals with out-of-town celebrities were also a spectator sport and major social events for the whole neighbourhood. The invited guest reclined facing into the area where the food was served. The rule was that anyone could show up to watch the meal and the discussion, but the uninvited guests stayed outside the circle formed by the invited guests' feet. For a known sinner to show up and to make such a scene as did the woman in this story was not unheard of. The real surprise is that Jesus allows it. And he does not just allow it, he also delights in it and forgives the woman for everything she has done, freely, completely. She can go in peace, unshackled by remorse, unencumbered by a sense of unworthiness, given a brand-new status and dignity as a beloved child of God. And that is a gift God offers to all of us, every one.

This is a difficult thing to accept. That we should go free, forgiven for all our sins, is tremendous. But often what is harder to accept is that it should be so for other people as well. Far too often we behave like Simon.

Jesus is the guest of a Pharisee. That means the house, the meal and everything connected to them was absolutely how it should be. And in return, Jesus should have been appropriately grateful and impressed. Instead he opens up the circle of invited guests to all and sundry – including known sinners. Worse still, he treats them as equal to the other guests. Simon, as a law-abiding Pharisee and host of the meal, feels justified in pointing this out to Jesus.

But instead of admitting his wrongdoing, Jesus somehow turns the tables on Simon. He points out to him the ways in which he failed to behave as a proper host should. This isn't a small-minded attack or a petty way of getting his own back; Jesus does this to make a broader point: when it comes to sharing a table with God, none of us are worthy. We cannot rely on our own credentials or righteousness to provide us with a seat. Not one of us can, not even if we point out to Jesus how much better behaved we are than our neighbour – particularly not if we do that!

Why might a sinner be closer to God than a Pharisee? Is it because the sinner has nothing to hide? The woman long ago cast aside the defences of self-righteousness and doublethink that so many of us erect rather than face the fact of our own sinfulness. She is free to approach Jesus just as she is, recognising her unworthiness, depending on his mercy.

The gospel message is simple – none of us are worthy, and all of us are invited. The source of our lives, the basis for our invitation into God's presence, is God's loving grace and forgiveness, nothing else. The gift to us of God's love is absolutely unearned, totally without merit and given freely to all.

God's love for us is absolute, total, unconditional and free. We cannot work our way into that love and we cannot sin our way out of it. We live by grace and forgiveness. Our lives as Christians are not about somehow managing to become loved or saved or accepted by God. It is not about taking an internet test and saying, 'Hooray! I haven't lied or stolen or sworn all day, I will get into heaven.' We have God's love already. We have been given that; we begin with that. Our lives as Christians are about responding to the gifts we have been given and learning to live with Jesus' words ringing in our ears as we determine to believe them, to live them and to share them: 'Your faith has saved you, go in peace.'

Questions

- If you were to take a test to see whether you would get into heaven or hell, what do you think you would score? Why do you think that?

- In what ways have you been a Pharisee today? How many sins are you prepared to acknowledge?

Prayer

Lord Jesus, so many times I have judged others today. So many times I have felt superior to somebody else. Help me not to set myself up above any of your children, but to approach you as one who is aware of my sin, forgiving of the sins of others and counting on your grace. Amen

Thursday 10 March

Living

Genesis 45:4–8; 50:15–21

Then Joseph said to his brothers, 'Come closer to me.' And they came closer. He said, 'I am your brother Joseph, whom you sold into Egypt. And now do not be distressed, or angry with yourselves, because you sold me here; for God sent me before you to preserve life. For the famine has been in the land these two years; and there are five more years in which there will be neither ploughing nor harvest. God sent me before you to preserve for you a remnant on earth, and to keep alive for you many survivors. So it was not you who sent me here, but God; he has made me a father to Pharaoh, and lord of all his house and ruler over all the land of Egypt...

Realising that their father was dead, Joseph's brothers said, 'What if Joseph still bears a grudge against us and pays us back in full for all the wrong that we did to him?' So they approached Joseph, saying, 'Your father gave this instruction before he died, "Say to Joseph: I beg you, forgive the crime of your brothers and the wrong they did in harming you." Now therefore please forgive the crime of the servants of the God of your father.' Joseph wept when they spoke to him. Then his brothers also wept, fell down before him, and said, 'We are here as your slaves.' But Joseph said to them, 'Do not be afraid! Am I in the place of God? Even though you intended to do harm to me, God intended it for good, in order to preserve a numerous people, as he is doing today. So have no fear; I myself will provide for you and your little ones.' In this way he reassured them, speaking kindly to them.

Reflection

There can be few scenes more touching than the one set before us in the first part of this passage. Joseph, once the favoured son, sold as a slave, imprisoned in an Egyptian jail, now Pharaoh's right-hand man, finally reveals himself to his brothers. These men, who have lived with their regret over the way they treated their young brother and the misery it has caused their father, have been punished in more ways than one. The country they live in is suffering from famine and they have come begging for food from their neighbour. Led, no doubt bewildered and unsure, to the centre of power, their shock when they finally recognised their long-lost brother must have been overwhelming. So too must have been the wave of fear which might well have swept over them as they realised that this man whom they had mistreated and thought dead all these years was not only alive but held their lives in his hands. But to their astonishment, Joseph does not seem to hold this against them, simply asserting that their actions were part of God's plans for him: 'It was not you who sent me here but God.'

What an amazingly graceful thing to say! Joseph has turned his years of unjust treatment, suffering and helplessness into a gift from God. Through the challenges of his life, he has become strong and resourceful. No longer is he the arrogant and boastful young man who told his brothers of his dreams of power – instead he is concerned with the bigger issue of saving his people from famine and ensuring the continuation of the line. In this speech, Joseph sets aside all bitterness and sense of loss and is able to see how God has worked in his life to fulfil God's purposes. What an example of lived forgiveness!

Or is it? Nowhere in this passage do we find those powerful words 'I forgive you'. Instead, Joseph reminds the brothers of their responsibility for all his suffering: 'I am your brother Joseph, whom you sold into Egypt.' Admittedly, this great wrong had a beneficial result, but still the wrong was committed, and Joseph has not forgotten that.

And we should not forget how much Joseph has manipulated and exploited his brothers before they arrive at this scene. The brothers have been accused of being spies and imprisoned, one of them being held captive while the others were sent back for Benjamin. Valuable goods were planted in their grain sacks and they have been accused of stealing, and Benjamin is threatened with slavery. Only when the meeting has reached a pitch of extreme anxiety and fear does Joseph disclose that he is their brother.

And still he does not forgive them. He has tested them to see if they are truly repentant of their actions against him – and he has proof that they are: 'They said to one another, "Surely we are being punished because of our brother. We saw how distressed he was when he pleaded with us for his life, but we would not listen; that's why this distress has come on us"' (Genesis 42:21, NIV).

But still he continues. More powerful still is the evidence that the brothers still fear Joseph, even after this scene of reconciliation. When Jacob dies, they fear that their father's presence was all that was holding Joseph back from retaliation, and they invent some deathbed words begging Joseph's forgiveness on behalf of the brothers. Only then, perhaps, does Joseph realise the power games he has been playing: 'Am I in the place of God?' Instead of continuing his manipulation of his brothers, he offers them reassurance and promises them an end to punishment.

Lived forgiveness does not involve testing those who offend against us to see if they are truly sorry for what they have done. Lived forgiveness does not involve constantly reminding others of the wrong they have committed, forcing them to apologise and make amends again and again. Lived forgiveness does not involve holding on to the wrong indefinitely. Lived forgiveness sets us, and those who offend against us, free. It is not until Joseph has let go of his anger and resentment against his brothers that he can truly forgive them and move forward. Only then can he look back at God's provision and look forward to a shared future: 'Don't be afraid. I will provide for you and your children.'

Questions

- At what stage in the story do you think Joseph truly forgives his brothers?
- How easy do you find it to see God's loving purposes in some of the things that have happened to you?
- Are there people in your life whose repentance you have tested? Are you still testing them?
- Are there people in your life whom you feel have not forgiven you?

Prayer

> If we really want to love, we must learn how to forgive.
> Mother Teresa (1910–97)

Heavenly Father, help me to forgive not just with my lips and my head, but also with my heart. Help me not to return to the wrongs which I have forgiven, but to lay them down and journey on unburdened by resentment. Help me to have faith in your good purposes for me, even when they remain a mystery to me. Help me to forgive and to love. Amen

Friday 11 March

Telling

John 4:16–30, 39–42

Jesus said to [the Samaritan woman], 'Go, call your husband, and come back.' The woman answered him, 'I have no husband.' Jesus said to her, 'You are right in saying, "I have no husband"; for you have had five husbands, and the one you have now is not your husband. What you have said is true!' The woman said to him, 'Sir, I see that you are a prophet. Our ancestors worshipped on this mountain, but you say that the place where people must worship is in Jerusalem.' Jesus said to her, 'Woman, believe me, the hour is coming when you will worship the Father neither on this mountain nor in Jerusalem. You worship what you do not know; we worship what we know, for salvation is from the Jews. But the hour is coming, and is now here, when the true worshippers will worship the Father in spirit and truth, for the Father seeks such as these to worship him. God is spirit, and those who worship him must worship in spirit and truth.' The woman said to him, 'I know that Messiah is coming' (who is called Christ). 'When he comes, he will proclaim all things to us.' Jesus said to her, 'I am he, the one who is speaking to you.'

Just then his disciples came. They were astonished that he was speaking with a woman, but no one said, 'What do you want?' or, 'Why are you speaking with her?' Then the woman left her water-jar and went back to the city. She said to the people, 'Come and see a man who told me everything I have ever done! He cannot be the Messiah, can he?' They left the city and were on their way to him...

Many Samaritans from that city believed in him because of the woman's testimony, 'He told me everything I have ever done.' So when the Samaritans came to him, they asked him to stay with them; and he stayed there for two days. And many more believed because of his word. They said to the woman, 'It is no longer because of what you said that we believe, for we have heard for ourselves, and we know that this is truly the Saviour of the world.'

Reflection

As part of my training for ordination, I went on a placement with an army regiment. It was a huge culture shock – not least because I spent a week living in the officers' mess, which was both baffling and entertaining. I was carelessly briefed by a young lieutenant on all the things I could and couldn't do and say, with the result that I spent quite a lot of my time apologising for inadvertent errors. Of course, the most obvious error, in those days, was my gender and my choice of occupation, both of which were considered a bit beyond the pale in the macho environment of that particular mess. Rereading today's story reminded me strongly of the feeling of being an outcast and of not belonging. Being forced to walk up two flights of stairs and along a corridor before I could find a woman's bathroom is a milder hardship than travelling to the well for water in the middle of the day, but I haven't forgotten that sense of being excluded and shut out.

For me, the experience was made worthwhile by my contact with the army chaplain. Despite being months away from retiring, he didn't mind in the least that he had to shepherd an inexperienced woman and was happy to spend precious time talking to me about the skills and craft of chaplaincy.

What made him memorable was his sheer joy in the privilege of being able to share the gospel with so many people. He told me that, as a youth, he was wild and unhappy, committing crimes and sins for which he and others still bore the scars. All that changed, however, when he went to a church meeting 'almost by accident – except that with God there are no accidents' and underwent a dramatic conversion. He turned his life around, studied, trained and joined the army so that he could minister to young men from a similar background to his. He brought to his ministry an endless patience and compassion and a loving understanding for the men in his care. Guiding everything he did was a compulsion to share the good news of Jesus' love for all people, whoever they were and whatever they had done. He wanted everyone to have the same experience he did – of a drowning man reaching for straws but finding instead a life-saving rock.

I am reminded of that chaplain when I read of the Samaritan woman. Cast out of normal society, she epitomises the marginalised and dispossessed. She has broken gender, purity, wealth, religion and moral taboos. But then she meets Jesus and her life is turned upside down. She is emboldened by his offering of inclusion to explore the nature of faith and forgiveness. Step by step she journeys to the heart of things and comes to believe that the living water, which quenches spiritual thirst and refreshes weary souls, is available to her through Christ.

Her transformation, however, runs deeper than mere personal acceptance. So overwhelmed is she with what she has discovered that she runs back to her community – that same community which pushed her to the fringes – to share her experience. The Samaritan has become an evangelist, a disciple. She has met someone who has understood her and not judged her, someone who sees what she is and what she has been and forgives all that, someone who has given her value and a belief in her future. No surprise that joy and wonder spill out of her, urging the entire village to encounter Jesus for themselves.

And the miracle is they do. People recognise the change in the woman and are eager to understand how this has come about. They believe in the transformation and are thus led to believe in the cause of that transformation: 'We know that this is truly the Saviour of the world.'

The unlikeliest of people can be evangelists. The strangest of stories can lead others to God. The most unsuitable speakers can pierce the hearts and souls of the lost and lead them to love. We must not judge the ability of others to speak the gospel; we must not limit ourselves or our capabilities. A heart overflowing with an experience of love, eager to share that experience in words and deeds, will be led by the Spirit to those who need to hear words of compassion and healing, light in darkness.

Questions

- What is your story of salvation? Have you ever shared it with anyone? If you did, what was the result? If you haven't yet, should you?

- The people in the village heard the good news from the woman first, but then they heard for themselves and believed. Do you rely too much on the testimony of others to support you in your faith? How could you drink more deeply of the living water which Jesus offers to us all?

- How open is your mind to the ways in which people can be saved? Is there a formula which should be used or are you brave enough to let the Spirit speak in strange and unexpected ways?

Prayer

Jesus, Saviour of the world, help me to drink more deeply of your living water. Help me to allow myself to be refreshed and energised by your life-enriching Spirit. Keep me from judgement of myself and others; lead me in the paths of forgiveness and compassion, so that I may be made whole and strong to do your work. Amen

Saturday 12 March

Sharing

Matthew 6:9–15

‘Pray then in this way:

Our Father in heaven,
hallowed be your name.
Your kingdom come.
Your will be done,
on earth as it is in heaven.
Give us this day our daily bread.
And forgive us our debts,
as we also have forgiven our debtors.
And do not bring us to the time of trial,
but rescue us from the evil one.

For if you forgive others their trespasses, your heavenly Father will also forgive you; but if you do not forgive others, neither will your Father forgive your trespasses.’

Reflection

Reflecting on my memories of the army chaplain I met so many years ago brought back more recollections from training days and the early years of ministry, when I worked with the British army as a civilian chaplain. I was fortunate enough to be able to accompany some soldiers on exercise, where I gained a fuller understanding of the nature and challenges of their work.

In those days, a soldier's kit was in three parts. The first was a large bergen or backpack, often weighing 22 kg or more, which contained everything needed to go on exercise. This heavy bag would remain in the soldier's quarters during the day, with all that was necessary for that day's activities transferred to a small daysack, which was carried easily on the back. However, the absolute essentials – the things the soldier didn't want to be without in any situation – went into the webbing, the set of straps and pouches which the soldier wore all day.

Thinking about this threefold set of kit helps me to picture the kit we use as Christians in our daily prayer life. First, there is the church, with its community and its worship offerings, its resources and teaching. As Christians, we need this community to help and support us as we in turn offer service to others. It is our bergen, if you like. Second, the Bible, with its stories and poems, prayers and histories, is needed by us all through the day, if not in physical form, then certainly in the way it guides and informs our words and actions. It is our daysack. Third, our webbing, our essentials, comes in a tightly packed emergency ration of prayer – that prayer the Lord himself taught us. Without that we are lost indeed; with it we have all that is necessary to listen and speak to God.

How interesting, therefore, that in Matthew's version of the Lord's Prayer, it is the lines about forgiveness that are explained further. Clearly this is a task and an obligation which is so important that not only does it form part of that essential Christian prayer, but it needs further explanation so that we truly understand the vital part it plays in all our lives.

Matthew understands that the human world is composed of a careful network of debt and obligation. From the earliest concept of bartering goods and services to the current complexities of banking and currency exchange, we offer and receive things of all kind in exchange for others. Social interactions are no less bound by give and take – even more so in some cultures. The carefully worked-out scale of favours sought and returned are what makes many family, friendship and social networks function smoothly and to mutual benefit. And it is an expected part of this framework that we should all be in debt to one degree or another in a variety of different ways: from the financial obligations placed upon us by mortgages and loans, to the social ones of babysitting, alternating hosting of meals, rounds in pubs and even turns on rotas. So, debt we understand.

Release from debt we understand too – that surge of joy when we receive something for which no return is expected. An anonymous gift, a spontaneous gesture of encouragement or support, the lifting of a burden of duty or care – these things surprise and delight. In kingdom terms, this gift is grace – an unmerited outpouring of forgiveness for all debts, enabling a fresh start, a new beginning, a slate wiped clean, which demands nothing in return.

Or does it? We are told that only when we forgive others will our debts be forgiven. How can this be when Jesus' death on the cross brought redemption for all because Jesus himself paid the price required? Is Matthew truly saying that forgiveness is transactional after all, simply a part of the exchange system of our fallen world? No, to think that is to forget that forgiveness is the saving work of God, part of the day-to-day work of Christ's operation in this world.

Perhaps what Matthew is reminding us of is that forgiveness, although freely given, is inextricably bound up with repentance. Unless we repent of our sinful actions, we cannot seek forgiveness. Unless we let go of the things that hold us back in our relationship with God – our selfishness, our lack of love, our clinging on to old resentments and past hurts – there will be no room for forgiveness.

The Lord's Prayer is our lifeblood, reminding us daily of the limitless gifts of God's love and grace, but also of the necessity to place ourselves constantly within the scope of that love – through faith, through prayer and through giving and receiving forgiveness.

Questions

- What would you put in your 'bergen of faith' and your 'daysack'? What would you add to your 'webbing' as well as the Lord's Prayer?
- You likely know the Lord's Prayer off by heart, able to reach for it in times of need. Are there other prayers you know by heart? Perhaps try to learn one or two more to keep in your 'kit'.

Prayer

He that cannot forgive others, breaks the bridge over which he himself must pass if he would ever reach heaven; for everyone has need to be forgiven.
George Herbert (1593–1633)

Heavenly Father, help me to build bridges of forgiveness. Let these bridges span my hurt and my grief so that I may walk boldly and with love into your presence. Amen

Sunday 13 March

Becoming

Luke 1:67–89

Then his father Zechariah was filled with the Holy Spirit and spoke this prophecy:

'Blessed be the Lord God of Israel,
for he has looked favourably on his people and redeemed them.
He has raised up a mighty saviour for us
in the house of his servant David,
as he spoke through the mouth of his holy prophets from of old,
that we would be saved from our enemies and from the hand of all who hate us.
Thus he has shown the mercy promised to our ancestors,
and has remembered his holy covenant,
the oath that he swore to our ancestor Abraham,
to grant us that we, being rescued from the hands of our enemies,
might serve him without fear, in holiness and righteousness
before him all our days.
And you, child, will be called the prophet of the Most High;
for you will go before the Lord to prepare his ways,
to give knowledge of salvation to his people
by the forgiveness of their sins.
By the tender mercy of our God,
the dawn from on high will break upon us,

to give light to those who sit in darkness and in the shadow of death,
to guide our feet into the way of peace.'

The child grew and became strong in spirit, and he was in the wilderness until the day he appeared publicly to Israel.

Reflection

Where does the story of salvation begin? For Mark, it begins when Jesus launches his ministry here on earth – at the moment of his baptism. John, however, takes the opposite approach, and we are taken right back before the beginning of time, assured that before everything, there was the Word, and that it was this eternal Word which took flesh and 'lived among us'. Matthew is concerned to demonstrate the righteous genealogy of Christ, part of a long line of children of Israel, bringing hope to the world.

For Luke, however, the main concern is to get the story right:

> With this in mind, since I myself have carefully investigated everything from the beginning, I too decided to write an orderly account for you, most excellent Theophilus, so that you may know the certainty of the things you have been taught.
> LUKE 1:3–4 (NIV)

So where does Luke start? Not with the birth of Christ, but with the birth of John, the prophet, the herald, the signpost.

John's story begins in silence. It is the silence of a man who thought he knew God, who thought he knew God's ways. Zechariah was a good, faithful priest who had served God all his life. He and his wife were childless, which, while not a great tragedy in the context of world events, was devastating for a loving couple with more love to give.

Childlessness meant economic hardship as well – there would be no one to look after the couple when they became ill or frail, no one to support Elizabeth if Zechariah died. But they have come to terms with their lot and all that it meant, and they accept the rhythms and seasons of life as God's will.

Until, that is, God himself comes to disrupt everything with a message from an angel. This message is so astounding, so outrageous, so contrary to the laws of nature that Zechariah questions it: 'How can I be sure of this? I am an old man and my wife is well on in years' (Luke 1:18, NIV). Gabriel thunders back his answer: for daring to question God, Zechariah is silenced.

Who knows what happened after that – the struggles of Zechariah to make himself understood; the incomprehension of Elizabeth on discovering her pregnancy; the agonies of a couple unable to communicate at such an important time. But silence is a blessing as well as a trial. During those long months, when the baby developed and grew, Zechariah must have had time to think. Time to think how he had put God in a box of human construction, limiting his powers and confining his sphere of action. Time to repent of his unbelief, time to grow in maturity of faith.

Elizabeth too spends the first five months of her pregnancy in seclusion, breaking her isolation only when Mary comes to stay for the first three months of her own pregnancy. Elizabeth's time alone has borne fruit – at Mary's appearance she recognises the wonderful thing that has happened, loudly exclaiming: 'Blessed are you among women, and blessed is the child you will bear! But why am I so favoured, that the mother of my Lord should come to me?' (Luke 1:42–43, NIV).

Zechariah's time of silence enables him to come to repentance – his tongue is loosed once that repentance has been made public and the child is named according to God's will. And Zechariah's first words are praise: 'Immediately his mouth was opened and his tongue set free, and he began to speak, praising God' (Luke 1:64, NIV).

This praise takes further shape into the wonderful poem known as the Benedictus, as the redemption of humankind is prophesied and the promise of forgiveness held out to all people. John's task will be to guide the feet of all who listen to him 'into the way of peace'. Zechariah's experience demonstrates what this way of peace will be – a way of humility, of a willingness to change, of perseverance, of listening for God in the silence. To find this way, to get on the path of righteousness, we need only repent and receive the forgiveness which is offered to us all through Christ. Then, through God's mercy, the path will be lit before us and we will be empowered to travel joyfully and fearlessly, wherever the way leads.

Questions

- How often do we put God in a box, limiting his powers by our own expectations?
- Has there been an occasion when God has surprised you by his power? What did you learn from that?

Prayer

Nine months for a mistrustful word,
nine months of silence must atone.
Charles Wesley (1707–88)

Father, forgive me when I doubt you; forgive me when I let fear overwhelm me and limit what I can do. Help me to worship you joyfully and faithfully through my words and actions, aware of your forgiving presence as I try to walk in your way of peace. Amen

Questions for group study

- Reflecting on this week's Bible passages, which ones have engaged you most? Which have you found most challenging? Has your understanding of forgiveness changed, and, if so, how?

- 'The kingdom of God is not a transactional arrangement.' Do you agree? What are the advantages and disadvantages of this?

- Which is the most important task – to feel forgiven or to forgive others? Which is the harder task for you?

 Creative prayer

You will need: a large shallow bowl, a candle, a jug of water, simple paper flower shapes, water-soluble felt-tip pens.

Fill the bowl with water.

Spend some time reflecting on the things in your past which need forgiveness. These might be great or small, recently committed or long ago.

Take your flower shape and write a few words in the centre of the shape with a water-soluble felt-tip pen.

Fold the petals over the centre so that they cover it.

Place the flower gently in the water. The petals will gradually unfold, revealing your sin, just as the actions of your heart are known to God.

Gradually, the water will cover the flower and wash away the writing.

Light the candle and thank God for his gift of forgiveness and promise of new life in Christ.

Week 3 | Monday 14 March–Sunday 20 March

Hoping

When I was young, one of my favourite books was an illustrated version of Pandora's box. The first woman created by Hephaestus on the orders of Zeus, Pandora was the bride of Epimetheus. A precious box was left in her care one day with instructions not to open it – which she disobeyed. Out from the box flew all the ills of the world – disease, hunger, famine. She went to shut the box but fortunately let out the last thing of all – hope.

The illustration for this event was a dark mass of chaotic figures swirling out of an ornate box and at the bottom, crouched in a corner, a frail, transparent wisp which was Hope. To this day, I see the hopes of the world as fragile, insubstantial beings, ready to be carried away by the slightest gust of wind. And this is probably an accurate description of all those things in which we tend to put our hopes – money, power, status, even people.

But the Bible shows us that the hope of God is not some will-o'-the-wisp but solid and mighty, powerful and completely dependable. It is a sign of things both here and yet to come, that 'sure and certain hope'.

We still need hope, because we still see 'through a glass, darkly' (1 Corinthians 13:12, KJV). But one day, we will see God face to face, and our hopes will be gloriously realised in Christ.

Monday 14 March

Listening

Jeremiah 29:1, 5–7, 10–14

These are the words of the letter that the prophet Jeremiah sent from Jerusalem to the remaining elders among the exiles, and to the priests, the prophets, and all the people, whom Nebuchadnezzar had taken into exile from Jerusalem to Babylon... Build houses and live in them; plant gardens and eat what they produce. Take wives and have sons and daughters; take wives for your sons, and give your daughters in marriage, that they may bear sons and daughters; multiply there, and do not decrease. But seek the welfare of the city where I have sent you into exile, and pray to the Lord on its behalf, for in its welfare you will find your welfare...

For thus says the Lord: Only when Babylon's seventy years are completed will I visit you, and I will fulfil to you my promise and bring you back to this place. For surely I know the plans I have for you, says the Lord, plans for your welfare and not for harm, to give you a future with hope. Then when you call upon me and come and pray to me, I will hear you. When you search for me, you will find me; if you seek me with all your heart, I will let you find me, says the Lord, and I will restore your fortunes and gather you from all the nations and all the places where I have driven you, says the Lord, and I will bring you back to the place from which I sent you into exile.

Reflection

My husband's grandmother was once asked what music she would choose to take with her if she was stranded on a desert island. Her response was swift and certain: 'I wouldn't go on a desert island!' This has become a family saying for those situations in which no solution is a good one, and it comes to mind when I read Jeremiah's instructions to the exiles in Babylon. They don't want to be on that desert island, but that is precisely where they are and they must decide how they are going to live in these circumstances and what music to play.

For years Jeremiah had been prophesying to the people of Jerusalem, warning them of disasters to come. Their own actions were bringing this about, their lack of care for the orphan and the widow, the sick and the poor of their community. For years no one listened – and then disaster did indeed strike. In 587BCE, Nebuchadnezzar overran the city of Jerusalem, destroyed the temple and carried off a large number of the population to live in exile in Babylon.

The children of Israel were distraught. What were they to do now? Where was God? Where were his mighty acts of power? How could he let this happen to them, his chosen ones, his children? There was a huge sense of grief and loss, not just for homes and neighbourhoods, occupations and relationships, but also for the rites and rituals of their faith, rippling out from the temple and all that it meant to them. For the Jewish people the geography of salvation was tied up inextricably with the holy city of Jerusalem, and the temple – the place where God dwelt on earth – was at the heart of this. And it was all destroyed. No wonder they 'sat and wept' by the rivers of Babylon (Psalm 137:1, NIV). Little surprise that when their captors demanded songs of joy they asked, 'How can we sing the songs of the Lord while in a foreign land?' (Psalm 137:4, NIV). Loss of faith was imminent; despair triumphed.

Jeremiah's response is loving but robust. Never afraid to tell it how it was, he reminded the children of Israel that they had brought this upon themselves, but he also gave them a plan of action, a direction to head in, even though it was not necessarily what they wanted to hear.

All anyone wants to hear when they are in the midst of a disaster is that it will not last, that soon things will be right and back to how they were. Jeremiah doesn't say this. Instead he warns the exiles that they are in it for the long game. They are not to sit around hoping the bad things will soon end; they are to settle down and make the best of what they have. Jeremiah instructs his people to build houses and plant gardens – things which can be left, although not easily. However, he also instructs them to marry, presumably not only each other but also the local population, to become family. This is truly long-term stuff. More significant still, the children of Israel are not to doubt God's presence with them in this strange land; they are instead to pray for its prosperity and for the prosperity of its people. They are to become truly integrated, dependent upon the well-being of the land for their own thriving.

His bracing words over, Jeremiah addresses his battered, frightened people with love and reassurance, offering them hope for both the long-term and the immediate future. Those who are adults now will never see Jerusalem restored, but future generations will, he promises. In the meantime, they must never forget God's presence, which is not dependent on the condition of the holy city or the existence of the temple. They have managed without it before, and they will manage now – their God is a travelling God, an eternal God, who is always within hearing distance of his children: 'When you call upon me and come and pray to me, I will hear you.'

When we are in the midst of disaster, when our lives have been turned upside down, the immediate and natural reaction is to wish that all was back to how it used to be. We might doubt the existence of a God who could allow pain and suffering to afflict us, who could leave us in exile from health or happiness, security or financial stability, isolated and alone. But God can be found wherever we are, and God's plans are for our 'welfare and not for harm', giving us a 'future with hope'.

Living in exile is not easy – it takes courage and perseverance, energy and optimism. The exile might be lifelong, but God's purposes will be fulfilled wherever we are, and it might be that his purposes for us are best worked out in exile. We are called to pray for the 'strange land' we find ourselves in, to work among its people, within each situation, and always to hope in God's kingdom.

Questions

- 'Nothing worth doing can be accomplished in a single lifetime... therefore we are saved by hope' (Reinhold Niebuhr, 1892–1971). What do you think of this quote? What do you think it means? How might it apply to your own situation?
- How might the experience of the Jewish people in exile in Babylon help us to be more understanding to those in exile in our own society – those afflicted by personal or national disaster, such as refugees and migrants?
- What 'music' raises your spirits when you find yourself on a 'desert island'?

Prayer

Lord of all, help us to remember your presence when we are in exile. As we search for you, let us find you. As we call upon you, hear us. Gather us from our scattered state and bring us into the glory of your kingdom. Amen

Tuesday 15 March

Understanding

Ephesians 1:15–19

I have heard of your faith in the Lord Jesus and your love towards all the saints, and for this reason I do not cease to give thanks for you as I remember you in my prayers. I pray that the God of our Lord Jesus Christ, the Father of glory, may give you a spirit of wisdom and revelation as you come to know him, so that, with the eyes of your heart enlightened, you may know what is the hope to which he has called you, what are the riches of his glorious inheritance among the saints, and what is the immeasurable greatness of his power for us who believe, according to the working of his great power.

Reflection

'Strength for today and bright hope for tomorrow', we ask in that wonderful hymn, so loved at funerals and memorial services. It is a reminder that, while all seems dark at the moment, better times will come; the pain will ease and joy will break once more through the sadness of our grief.

The Ephesians were certainly in need of hope. This small group of Jews and Gentiles, gathered together in a Mediterranean fishing port, were facing some challenging times. Immediately after the death and resurrection of Christ, the promise of the second coming shone brightly for all who believed that Jesus was the Messiah, the Son of

God. Christians looked forward to the imminent arrival of the kingdom, the 'new Jerusalem', which was promised to all believers.

But as time wore on and that first generation of believers began to grow old and die without the vision being made real, doubts began to set in. The life of a Christ-follower looked to be a lonely, fear-filled one, with the prospect of persecution or imprisonment a very real threat. The founder and leader of their community, Paul himself, had already suffered beatings and imprisonment – was this all that lay ahead for them? So, yes, there was a real need among the saints at Ephesus to 'know what is the hope to which he has called you'.

And Paul was certainly the man to offer it – Paul, who joyfully suffered all the adversities which his calling as missionary and evangelist thrust upon him; Paul, who declared a few dozen people in a shabby fishing port a 'new community'; Paul, who saw these men and women as carrying out the sacramental work of reconciliation on behalf of Christ.

But it is not enough for us, as it probably wasn't enough for the Ephesians, to know that we are part of a bigger plan, that the second coming may not happen within our lifetimes, that although we are heralds of the kingdom, we probably won't witness its arrival. 'Some day' sometimes isn't strong enough; we need help to get us through 'this day'. So Paul offers us hope today, hope lighting up the here and now, illuminating the greatness of God's power, reminding us that the kingdom is both now and not yet, and that signs of this kingdom lie all around us. We just need to open our eyes to see.

Hope is not always easy – it challenges us, bidding us to move out of our comfortable zone of despair, that grey sludge which covers the brightest thing with its mess of apathy and inertia. Hope encourages us to look beyond our current circumstances, to imagine a better, brighter future, and then to work towards making that vision a reality. Hope reminds us that God isn't finished with us yet – even though we might feel we have more or less finished with God!

Thomas Aquinas (1225–74) wrote that while ‘faith has to do with things that are not seen’, hope has to do with ‘things that are not yet at hand’. Hope is a calling, a vocation, sometimes an act of will, especially when our world has been darkened by suffering or grief, loss or pain. But the Spirit is always there, revealing the works of God, ‘enlightening’ the eyes of our heart so that we can see our future as children of God.

One of my favourite poems is ‘“Hope” is the thing with feathers’, by Emily Dickinson, which compares hope to a small bird perched in our soul, singing a ‘tune without the words’, offering ceaseless comfort and reassurance and never asking for a ‘crumb’ in return. Hope is like the feather in the trunk of Dumbo the elephant, the Disney cartoon character – the one he believes helps him fly, until one day the feather isn’t there and Dumbo realises that he can fly anyway. Hope is no longer needed, because the dream has become real.

Questions

- Emily Dickinson described hope as ‘the thing with feathers’. How helpful is that as a description? How would you describe hope?
- What gives you hope?

Prayer

'Hope' is the thing with feathers
That perches in the soul,
And sings the tune without the words,
And never stops at all,

And sweetest in the gale is heard;
And sore must be the storm
That could abash the little bird
That kept so many warm.

I've heard it in the chillest land,
And on the strangest sea;
Yet, never, in extremity,
It asked a crumb of me.

'"Hope" is the thing with feathers' by Emily Dickinson (1830–86)

Wednesday 16 March

Reflecting

Psalm 33:18–22

Truly the eye of the Lord is on those who fear him,
  on those who hope in his steadfast love,
to deliver their soul from death,
  and to keep them alive in famine.
Our soul waits for the Lord;
  he is our help and shield.
Our heart is glad in him,
  because we trust in his holy name.
Let your steadfast love, O Lord, be upon us,
  even as we hope in you.

Reflection

If you decide to shoulder your backpack, say goodbye to friends and loved ones and set off by foot on a pilgrimage, many adventures await you. There is the excitement over whether you will find a bed at the hostel you are aiming for – and whether that bed is in a 40-strong dormitory or a tiny attic just big enough for you and one other. There is the state of constant vigilance you must adopt over the well-being of your feet and legs – one infected blister or wrenched ankle can cause days of soreness. There is the joyful anticipation of mealtimes – whether taken alone under the shade of a tree or in the company of other pilgrims at the end of a long day of walking.

However, these all pale into insignificance besides the challenge of route-finding. Every long-distance route has its own distinct signage, whether it is the cockle shell directing you to Santiago de Compostela in Spain, the long-skirted pilgrim of the Via Francigena or the elaborate cross of St Olav's Way in Norway. Each route is marked with these signs, and searching for the next waymark becomes a vital part of the journey. If you are navigating by map, then the sign shows that you are on the right track; if you are dependent on the path alone, the sign is even more important. If you stray off course, there is no option other than to return to where you saw the last sign, and begin again from there.

Some of my most joyous moments on pilgrimage have occurred when finally I have spotted a reassuring sign after miles of uncertainty. One of my most treasured memories is of arriving at a crossroads in an obscure Spanish town and wondering uncertainly which way to go. Moments later, I was shouted at by half a dozen coffee-drinkers on a café terrace, waving their arms and pointing at the yellow shell sign on the wall above their heads.

Psalm 33, like so many of the psalms, reminds us of all that God has done for us. Not content merely with recalling the events of the escape from Egypt, we are taken right back to the beginning of time: 'By the word of the Lord the heavens were made, and all their host by the breath of his mouth' (v. 6). We are left in no doubt as to why we owe God our praise and worship: 'For he spoke, and it came to be; he commanded, and it stood firm' (v. 9). Surely one so powerful that he can contain the seas in a bottle and bring the counsel of nations to nothing can be trusted to watch over us! We praise God for who he is, not what he does – and we trust that he is watching over us: 'The Lord looks down from heaven; he sees all humankind' (v. 13).

There will be times when it seems as if the Lord is absent, when what we want to happen shows no sign of coming about, when we appear to be plunged into the doldrums of inactivity or when we are helpless to act and feel abandoned. Then we must not let our hearts fail, but instead trust in God and his good purposes for us. Even though it seems as if all is hopeless, we must continue to hope.

It is at these times that signposts are so helpful. As we look back into the events of our past, we will see, strung out like bright waymarks, the times and places when we have been aware of God's presence, when we have witnessed God's saving action in the world and when we have been reassured of his love for us. The memories of these times are precious to us; we should gather them to our hearts and treasure them, allowing their brightness to illuminate our onward path, letting their light show up the waymarks of our future direction so that we continue to travel in the sure and certain hope of God's good purposes for us.

And all the while, God is watching over us – perhaps hoping in turn that, rather than wait for him to change the world, we will act in his name and change it ourselves: 'From where he sits enthroned he watches all the inhabitants of the earth – he who fashions the hearts of them all, and observes all their deeds' (vv. 14–15).

Questions

- What have been the 'signposts' of God's love for you in the past? What signposts are you looking for right now?

- God has put his hope in us – how might you justify that hope? How might you 'sing a new song' in praise of God?

Prayer

Hope, like the gleaming taper's light,
adorns and cheers our way;
and still, as darker grows the night,
emits a brighter ray.
Oliver Goldsmith (1728–74)

Lord Jesus Christ, light of the world, help me to see with the eyes of hope, that I might witness to your light. Amen

Thursday 17 March

Living

1 Corinthians 13:1–7

If I speak in the tongues of mortals and of angels, but do not have love, I am a noisy gong or a clanging cymbal. And if I have prophetic powers, and understand all mysteries and all knowledge, and if I have all faith, so as to remove mountains, but do not have love, I am nothing. If I give away all my possessions, and if I hand over my body so that I may boast, but do not have love, I gain nothing.

Love is patient; love is kind; love is not envious or boastful or arrogant or rude. It does not insist on its own way; it is not irritable or resentful; it does not rejoice in wrongdoing, but rejoices in the truth. It bears all things, believes all things, hopes all things, endures all things.

Reflection

As a parish priest I have taken a number of weddings over the years, and I never fail to be moved by them. The crowded church, filled with family and friends, the meetings and introductions, the laughter, the photographs – and of course the couple themselves, so full of love and hope for the future. Naturally it is the unusual weddings that stand out in my mind – the one in the ruins of a chapel halfway up a mountain in Scotland; the one where the bride and groom held a child each, with two more hanging on to their clothes; the couple in their 80s, who had found love once more and whose faces shone with the joy of it all.

Many times I have had the privilege of being asked to baptise the children of these marriages, as the love felt between a couple extended outwards into the next generation. But this makes it all the more ironic that this most popular and well-loved reading for weddings wasn't originally intended for this purpose at all. The apostle Paul is not addressing two people who have decided to place their chances of happiness in the hands of another, trusting their hope in the future together, and who have come together to celebrate the start of this new way of life in God's presence. Rather, he is writing to a community of new Christians who have not spent a lot of time together but who are finding even that short amount of time rather trying.

The Corinthians Christians were a diverse bunch, to their credit. All sorts of people had come to believe in Christ as Messiah and were engaged in journeying along the Way together. There were married and single people, men, women and children, Jews and Gentiles. Their social status was equally varied – rich and poor, slaves and free – so it's hardly surprising that there were tensions. Paul was addressing the temptation felt by the Corinthians to gather in smaller groups, to cluster with similar, like-minded people, whose views were the same and who wanted the same things. This had naturally led to competition and division between the different groupings, and conflict and friction was imminent.

Paul acknowledges that love is indeed challenging, but that should not stop us aspiring to it. Love has many aspects, all of which require energy and engagement. We are not meant to be like the guests at a wedding – beautifully dressed and fairly well-behaved onlookers, content merely to observe the action at the front. We need to be part of that action, willing to get involved in the challenging and difficult business of loving. What makes it harder is that we are to love not just the people whom we find acceptable and agreeable, people whom it is easy to love; we are to love the unlovable, the prickly and the downright unpleasant, those who make our lives harder as well as those whose presence fills us with joy.

How do we do this? How do we achieve this impossible thing, to love in the way Paul tells us, with patience, kindness and humility, with forbearance, selflessness and forgiveness? Clearly we cannot do this on our own, but only through Christ, with grace and the Holy Spirit. This is where the trinity of faith, hope and love that Paul describes begins to operate – we can only love in and with faith. Believing that we are each of us loved by God, cherished for who we are, valued as individuals, we can in turn love others in the same way, appreciating their gifts and forgiving their faults as we trust God overlooks ours.

And tying faith and love together is that precious, fragile gift of hope – hope that a bride and groom will be able to partner each other through life's triumphs and tragedies; hope that a small, diverse community will learn how to live together, accepting and valuing difference while acknowledging that all are on the same path, looking towards the same eternity.

Questions

- Which have you found to be most important in your life – faith, hope or love? How would you describe each of them?

- What are your experiences of being in community – whether in your church or neighbourhood? How might that community be improved? How might you help to enable that improvement?

Prayer

'It's always something, to know you've done the most you could. But, don't leave off hoping, or it's of no use doing anything. Hope, hope to the last!'

Nicholas Nickleby by Charles Dickens (1812–70)

Heavenly Father, help me to keep hoping. Send your Spirit to me, so that I might see reasons to hope where others see only darkness. Fill me with your love, so that I may look with hope on the deeds of others. Give me faith to keep believing in your good plans for all people. Amen

Friday 18 March

Telling

1 Thessalonians 1:2–3; 4:13–18

> We always give thanks... constantly remembering before our God and Father your work of faith and labour of love and steadfastness of hope in our Lord Jesus Christ...
>
> But we do not want you to be uninformed, brothers and sisters, about those who have died, so that you may not grieve as others do who have no hope. For since we believe that Jesus died and rose again, even so, through Jesus, God will bring with him those who have died. For this we declare to you by the word of the Lord, that we who are alive, who are left until the coming of the Lord, will by no means precede those who have died. For the Lord himself, with a cry of command, with the archangel's call and with the sound of God's trumpet, will descend from heaven, and the dead in Christ will rise first. Then we who are alive, who are left, will be caught up in the clouds together with them to meet the Lord in the air; and so we will be with the Lord forever. Therefore encourage one another with these words.

Reflection

One of the joys of writing books such as these, books which require a close and careful study of Bible passages, is that even now, after many years of reading and studying the Bible, I come across things which I have not noticed before and continue to receive new insights into our faith. Sometimes these insights occur because the way that

I am looking at the passage has changed. This change might be due to external circumstances – the pandemic made lots of people look at the Bible with new eyes, as our world was thrown into confusion and old ways of living made way for new. The change might also be because my own circumstances have changed, and I am now reading the Bible through a lens of experience which causes different words and phrases to stand out.

This is one of the joys not just of Bible study, but also of trying to deepen and grow our faith as a whole. Based on the living Word, the message of the Bible is constantly changing and refreshing so that it is always able to meet the demands and uncertainties of the current situation with compassion and strength. And beneath this adaptability, the way in which this book is always able to speak into the present moment, there is the eternal rock of God's power and love, upon which we will always find certainty.

Looking at today's passage in the light of yesterday's, I am struck by one thing: in 1 Corinthians 13, Paul writes about 'faith, hope and love', trying to impress upon his fractious community the need to overcome differences of background and personal preference to unite in their goal of living out the gospel together. Today, however, Paul has written to the Thessalonians, and his message is slightly different. He praises them for all they have already done and the way in which they serve God in community. He commends them in their 'work produced by *faith*, your labour prompted by *love*, and your endurance inspired by *hope* in our Lord Jesus Christ' (v. 3, NIV, my italics). The order of that great trinity has been changed around! No longer is love the imperative, but hope, and it is hope which Paul entreats the Thessalonians to find and nurture in their situation.

As with the Corinthians, the community at Thessalonika was beginning to come to terms with the fact that the second coming, the new kingdom, would not come upon them as quickly as they originally supposed. Communities of Christians are in it for the long haul, and their faith must seek to make sense of this. Particularly distressing for the community Paul addresses here is the death of some of the members of the community. It had been supposed that the second coming, swift upon the heels of the death and resurrection of Christ, would not necessitate dealing with death, but this is not the case. If not through persecution and imprisonment, then illness and old age were having their effect upon the community, and they were concerned and bewildered. What would happen at the parousia, the second coming, to those who were already dead?

To put this concern in context, it must be remembered that the common belief about death at that time was that it was the absolute end of all things. A gravestone inscription of the time reads 'After death, no reviving; after the grave, no meeting again', echoing the philosophy of the Greek Epicurus: 'I was not, I became, I am not, I care not.'

How then to instil hope into the fragile new community of believers? In beautiful, poetic imagery, Paul describes to his anxious fellow Christians the moment of God's triumph, when with 'a cry of command, with the archangel's call and with the sound of God's trumpet', first those who are already dead, then the living will be caught up into heaven. Christ's death and resurrection have overturned old ways of thinking about death. Because of his saving action, Christ has opened a way through death for all of us, and in doing so has given us hope.

These joyful words echo through the centuries, reassuring each of us as we face our own moments of grief and anxiety at the death of a loved one. Uncertainty, doubt and loss of faith will assail us, as the reality sinks in of living without those whose lives we have shared and who have given us so much. Nor does Paul dismiss our natural feelings of sorrow – we are not told to not grieve, only to not grieve 'as others do who have no hope'. And he shares with us a fundamental of faith, in a phrase which is declaimed at the beginning of many funeral services today, reminding each of us that although we mourn, yet we can hope: 'For since we believe that Jesus died and rose again, even so, through Jesus, God will bring with him those who have died.'

Questions

- Reflect on your own experiences of mourning and grief. Did you find hope in its midst? If so, where was this hope to be found?
- Command, call and trumpet – Paul's poetic vision of the end of time is energetic and triumphant. Does this match your vision?

Prayer

Heavenly Father, we feel battered and bruised by grief, torn apart by memories of loved ones we see no more. Comfort and support us with an awareness of your presence, so that while we may grieve, we do not do so without hope. Amen

Saturday 19 March

Sharing

1 Thessalonians 2:17–20

As for us, brothers and sisters, when, for a short time, we were made orphans by being separated from you – in person, not in heart – we longed with great eagerness to see you face to face. For we wanted to come to you – certainly I, Paul, wanted to again and again – but Satan blocked our way. For what is our hope or joy or crown of boasting before our Lord Jesus at his coming? Is it not you? Yes, you are our glory and joy!

Reflection

Autumn 2019 was a good time for our church. I had been in post for over four years, and the congregation and I were getting to know each other and appreciate how we each worked. A good number of people attended church each Sunday, and we had a full programme of events, both social and educational. Our Messy Church was popular and valued by all generations, and the Sunday Club was small but supportive and enthusiastic. There was room for improvement, to be sure, but as I said to a senior member of the diocese who had visited the church for a service one Sunday, there was much to be joyful about.

Then coronavirus hit us, and our precious, loving, supportive congregation was scattered, each to their separate homes, locked down and isolated, a community no longer. We did all that we could to stay in touch – live-streamed services, daily reflections, prayer bags, and frequent emails and phone calls. But it was not the same, and I felt as if we were fractured and broken, the loving kindness which was at the heart of our community strained and often absent. Something had withered in the isolation, starved of accidental meetings in church, quick exchanges during coffee time, longer conversations during the regular café and other social events. I felt forlorn and mourned my optimistic mood of the autumn before.

But even amid the rules and the restrictions, the limitations and deprivation, the seeds of something new was growing. The inspiration was provided by a handful of people whose hearts were bigger than average, hands more open and generous, ideas and visions larger and more creative. An empty property was rented and decorated and a hub for giving and receiving was begun. Originally a response to a growing number of people who were finding it hard to feed their family in a time of joblessness, Cornerstone developed into a place where surplus could be donated and shortages made up. Excess produce from people's gardens and allotments; used books, toys and games; outgrown school uniforms with plenty of life left in them – all these things flowed into the Cornerstone, and out again.

All types of people used the Cornerstone, removing any stigma. Recipes involving quinces were swapped, and fresh eggs from overproductive hens eagerly seized upon. Other organisations began to look to Cornerstone as an outlet for their giving, whether fresh meals or information on funding or resourcing. Staffed by paid and voluntary workers, it became a place to meet and chat, giving and receiving so much more than was originally imagined, a symbol of what could be achieved if a community worked together.

Had it not been for the lockdown, Cornerstone would probably not have happened. Had our old way of doing things not been broken, we would not have found this new way of loving God through serving our community. As I write, we are still in the throes of Covid-19, so my story is unfinished; I do not know what its future will be. But I have learnt that even when things look dark indeed, God is still at work. Even when it seemed that all we had built together was falling apart, something better was being formed in the hearts and minds of a community which tried to put loving God and loving their neighbour into practice.

Paul's letter to the Thessalonians is full of longing – he wishes so much to see his small community again; he has been prevented by his persecutors from returning to Thessalonika, and it is doubtful whether this will ever be achieved. But he can rejoice in all that they are, this faithful, loving community who seek to follow Christ wherever this path leads. And he can put his hope in them – hope for their future as Christians and all that they will do and be. By sharing this hope, it will encourage and energise them, spurring them on to live more fully in the light of Christ. By sharing our hopes for each other and our communities, we can plant seeds of new life, nurture them and see them grow into something beautiful. If we can change just a small part of a small group into something better, this will truly be our glory and our joy.

Questions

- What has enabled you to keep hoping, even when 'Satan has blocked your way'?
- Is there something in your life which is your 'glory and joy'? Celebrate this, and thank God!

Prayer

When by my solitary hearth I sit,
And hateful thoughts enwrap my soul in gloom
When no fair dreams before my 'mind's eye' flit,
And the bare heath of life presents no bloom;
Sweet Hope, ethereal balm upon me shed,
And wave thy silver pinions o'er my head.

'To Hope' by John Keats (1795–1821)

Lord Jesus Christ, help me to place my hopes in you and your saving action for all people. Help me to have hope for myself and my community, and show me how I can turn hope into reality. Amen

Sunday 20 March

Becoming

Hebrews 6:13–20

> When God made a promise to Abraham, because he had no one greater by whom to swear, he swore by himself, saying, 'I will surely bless you and multiply you.' And thus Abraham, having patiently endured, obtained the promise. Human beings, of course, swear by someone greater than themselves, and an oath given as confirmation puts an end to all dispute. In the same way, when God desired to show even more clearly to the heirs of the promise the unchangeable character of his purpose, he guaranteed it by an oath, so that through two unchangeable things, in which it is impossible that God would prove false, we who have taken refuge might be strongly encouraged to seize the hope set before us. We have this hope, a sure and steadfast anchor of the soul, a hope that enters the inner shrine behind the curtain, where Jesus, a forerunner on our behalf, has entered, having become a high priest forever according to the order of Melchizedek.

Reflection

When my children were young, some of their favourite storybooks were Bel Mooney's series about a little girl called Kitty. Hers was not an adventurous life, just the ordinary round of school, swimming lessons, trips to the shops and outings with friends. But each book in the series dealt with an issue of growing up, exploring it from different angles and gently encouraging the reader/listener to engage with the concept and come to some understanding of its complexities. Together we read through *I Don't Want To!*, *It's Not Fair!*, *It's Not My Fault!* and *I'm Bored!*, but my favourite one was *But You Promised!*

In this book, Kitty experiences some of the many ways in which people, and life, can disappoint by failing to live up to their promises. Kitty's friend chooses another child to be on her team, Kitty is promised a dog but then her mother changes her mind, and her father promises Kitty that the injection won't hurt. Most poignant of all is the last chapter, in which Kitty's parents are unable to keep the promise they made that her grandmother would recover from her illness. The little girl accuses her parents of breaking their promise, to which the father sadly replies: 'When grown-ups say I promise, they often mean I hope.'

Our lives are littered with broken promises and abandoned hopes. Companies promise that our lives will improve if we only purchase their product. Politicians promise that our society will improve if we only give them our votes. Financial institutions promise a life of comfort if we only invest as they suggest. When it comes to relationships, we are surrounded by evidence of promises not kept, from boardroom backstabbing to marital infidelity, sibling betrayal to disloyal friends. If we are not careful, we might easily lose all hope and sink into a morass of despair and pessimism.

The people addressed in the letter to the Hebrews faced such challenges on an even greater scale. Initially enthusiastic upholders of their new faith in Jesus Christ, the Messiah, they are soon forced to confront the reality of such belief as they encounter incredible hardship and persecution. How can they endure such oppression? What is there to hope for amid difficulties and danger?

It might seem as if the writer of the letter is simply exhorting them to ever greater feats of endurance, as they try to screw their courage to the sticking place simply by force of will. But even the most determined endurance will not be sufficient, and is indeed wrong, as it implies a reliance on works rather than faith. So the writer reminds their anxious Christian listeners that their endurance is based on hope, and that hope comes from the promises made by God to each one of us.

These are not the fragile, conditional promises that fallible, sinful human beings make to each other in the context of a flawed and broken world. These are promises reinforced generation by generation, promises made to Abraham time and again as he left the land of this birth and struck out into the wilderness to seek a new land; as he believed in the gift of a son born from his wife Sarah; as he passed that greatest of all tests of faith in his willingness to sacrifice that son, Isaac, to the living God.

Abraham is not perfect, and his lapses from faith are well documented – his fear is so great that he offers his wife as a concubine; his lack of faith in God's promises results in the birth of Ishmael to Hagar. But this doesn't matter. God's promises are unchangeable and eternal. Any hope based on them has a sure foundation indeed.

These are Old Testament promises. Yet in the birth, death and resurrection of Christ, all these promises, all the covenants made between God and his people, are fulfilled. The promise has already been kept – our hope is now 'sure and certain'. This hope is stronger than a mere cheerful optimism and longer lasting than a grim-faced attitude of endurance. It is a steady attitude of joyful certainty that the endgame has already been played and we are all winners.

God promises; we hope in those promises. Our hope is not a vain one, built on an insubstantial longing or a flimsy foundation. It is placed in Jesus Christ, our rock, our redeemer. It has already been fulfilled. We simply need to believe that and live accordingly.

Questions

- It is easy to think of times when promises made to us or by us have been broken. Spend some time instead thinking of those times when promises have been kept, and celebrate them.

- What gives you hope? How might you give hope to others?

Prayer

Heavenly Father, keep alive the flame of hope in my heart, even when darkness threatens to extinguish it. Help me to believe in your promises and to build my life on the rock of your eternal love. Amen

Questions for group study

- Reflecting on this week's Bible passages, which ones have engaged you most? Which have you found most challenging? Has your understanding of hope changed, and, if so, how?

- Hope has been described as something which helps us focus on difficult goals. How helpful is that as a description?

- What seed of hope would you like to see planted in your community, your family, your heart? How can you nurture it?

Creative prayer

There is a trend for people in love to inscribe their initials on a padlock and fasten it to a bridge in a romantic spot. The danger with this is that there is a real possibility the padlock will outlast the relationship! Too many padlocks can also damage the bridge. Our relationship with God suffers no such dangers – his love for us will outlast time, and we can rest secure that the weight of our dependence upon him will be easily borne.

Attach a padlock to your prayer space, such as to the leg of a chair, a door handle or a window catch. Place it somewhere eye-catching, so that it will regularly remind you of the hope you have in Christ and the security of his promises.

Week 4 | Monday 21 March–Sunday 27 March

Trusting

There are times when I fear that trust has become a disposable virtue in today's world. The media is full of incidents of people trusting in the wrong institutions, the wrong groups, the wrong individuals – those who lie or cheat, those who betray the trust of others for financial gain. To be fair, the media is partly responsible for this untrustworthiness, as through the media all the frailties of human beings can be revealed instantly and ubiquitously. Nevertheless, our family lives and those of our communities and wider society are built on trust – trust that the food we buy is not rotten, that the banking establishments we use are sound, that our health services will do the best they can for us. When trust vanishes, the result is damaging and unhappy.

The Bible enables us to explore what it is to trust another human being, and what results when that trust is broken. But it goes further, and demonstrates time and again that if we place our trust in God, that will never be broken. Even when it seems as if our lives are shattered and that nothing we know can be relied upon, God's love for us remains as solid as ever – all we need to do is rest in it.

Monday 21 March

Listening

2 Kings 5:1–3, 9–15

Naaman, commander of the army of the king of Aram, was a great man and in high favour with his master, because by him the Lord had given victory to Aram. The man, though a mighty warrior, suffered from leprosy. Now the Arameans on one of their raids had taken a young girl captive from the land of Israel, and she served Naaman's wife. She said to her mistress, 'If only my lord were with the prophet who is in Samaria! He would cure him of his leprosy'...

So Naaman came with his horses and chariots, and halted at the entrance of Elisha's house. Elisha sent a messenger to him, saying, 'Go, wash in the Jordan seven times, and your flesh shall be restored and you shall be clean.' But Naaman became angry and went away, saying, 'I thought that for me he would surely come out, and stand and call on the name of the Lord his God, and would wave his hand over the spot, and cure the leprosy! Are not Abana and Pharpar, the rivers of Damascus, better than all the waters of Israel? Could I not wash in them, and be clean?' He turned and went away in a rage. But his servants approached and said to him, 'Father, if the prophet had commanded you to do something difficult, would you not have done it? How much more, when all he said to you was, "Wash, and be clean"?' So he went down and immersed himself seven times in the Jordan, according to the word of the man of God; his flesh was restored like the flesh of a young boy, and he was clean.

Then he returned to the man of God, he and all his company; he came and stood before him and said, 'Now I know

that there is no God in all the earth except in Israel; please accept a present from your servant.'

Reflection

There can be no doubt that the main character in this story is Naaman. Naaman, of the high social standing, the military success, the might and the power… and the skin disease. Although several translations use the word 'leprosy', there is no certainty that it was actually Hansen's disease. Whatever afflicted Naaman, it caused him great distress. So great, in fact, that he was prepared to undertake all sorts of humiliating actions and grasp at all sorts of straws on the off-chance that one of them might lead to a cure.

So Naaman listens to the words of his wife's servant and prepares to chase the rumour of a prophet in Samaria who might heal him. Naaman is willing to make use of his good standing with the king to gain permission to travel into Israel to seek this prophet. Although a supplicant, he retains some dignity as the kings correspond with each other to enable this to happen, and the gift from the king of Aram to the king of Israel is sizeable. But even this small portion of dignity cannot be maintained, and the action which Elisha's messenger (another humiliation) instructs Naaman to undertake requires even more self-abasement. To wash in the river of a conquered land, little more than a stream, really, necessitates the setting aside of all power and status, all the dignity gained by wealth and strength. Naked and humble, only then does Naaman find healing.

We might praise Naaman for having the courage to trust the word of a slave girl and to act upon the instructions of a prophet in a defeated land, but it seems to be courage born of desperation rather than conviction. Naaman had not been able to find a cure anywhere; isolation and social ostracism threatened – who knows what bizarre ritual he might have seized upon? But God does not close his ears to our entreaties, even if they arise from desperation. Many people have come to faith in the same way as Naaman.

A common saying when reflecting on faith during times of crisis is: 'There are no atheists in foxholes.' This saying perhaps originates from a comment by Hannah More in the 19th century: 'Under circumstances of distress, indeed, prayer is adopted with comparatively little reluctance; the mind, which knows not where to fly, flies to God. In agony, nature is no Atheist.' Rescued from disaster, witnesses to God's power, we can all acknowledge that 'there is no God in all the earth except in Israel'. We should not be ashamed if our trust is first placed in God in extremis, provided that we build on that first encounter, exploring and studying, praying and growing in faith until our trust has strong roots, a solid foundation. God does not despise anyone who seeks him, and he waits patiently until we allow him entry into our souls, where his healing work can truly begin:

> Listen! I am standing at the door, knocking; if you hear my voice and open the door, I will come in to you and eat with you, and you with me.
>
> REVELATION 3:20

And what of that other, much more minor character – the slave girl? She is the one who first plants the seed of Naaman's salvation in his mind. She is the one who points the way to healing and faith. Her words set Naaman on his journey. We don't know much about her, except that she was captured when Israel was defeated by the Arameans and set to work as a slave for the wife of Naaman. We don't even know her name – but we do know about her faith and her trust in God. There are echoes here of Joseph, who, even in the darkest times, continued to pray and to place his trust in his creator (Genesis 39).

Whether we have great might and power, social status and political significance or are very ordinary indeed, hardly worthy of a mention in the annals of history, we all have a part to play in the story of salvation. Whether our trust in God is that of desperation, when all else has failed, or remains strong and steadfast despite all hardships and challenges, that trust matters. We must open our hearts to the words of God, being prepared to listen for them, whatever their source, and we must place our future in the hands of the one who truly has all the power.

Questions

- Whose faith is most inspirational for you – Naaman's or the girl's?
- Do you agree that 'there are no atheists in foxholes'?

Prayer

Trust in the Lord with all your heart
    and lean not on your own understanding;
in all your ways submit to him,
    and he will make your paths straight.
PROVERBS 3:5–6 (NIV)

Father of all, help me to place my trust in you, even when it seems as if my paths are far from straight. Give me courage to rely upon you, and hope that my trust will be rewarded. Amen

Tuesday 22 March

Understanding

Titus 1:7–9

For a bishop, as God's steward, must be blameless; he must not be arrogant or quick-tempered or addicted to wine or violent or greedy for gain; but he must be hospitable, a lover of goodness, prudent, upright, devout and self-controlled. He must have a firm grasp of the word that is trustworthy in accordance with the teaching, so that he may be able both to preach with sound doctrine and to refute those who contradict it.

Reflection

One of my most poignant memories is talking to a retired priest at the induction of his successor to his final group of parishes. For over 40 years this priest had carried out his ministry, all of it except his curacy undertaken in rural parishes. With numerous churches grouped together in one or more parishes or benefices, he had led countless church council meetings, hosted dozens of fundraising events, managed several major building projects and installed a number of toilets. He had baptised babies, given Sunday school talks, held confirmation lessons, married those same babies and buried their parents. And Sunday after Sunday he had faithfully preached the gospel, even as he tried to live out its precepts during the rest of the week. His home was always open, his day off frequently sacrificed, his own wishes put second to the demands of his churches and their communities.

I spoke to him as he stood in the garden of what had been his home and was now the home of another, and asked him how he felt about it all. 'Well', he said, 'I survived.' Then he paused, as if aware that these two words completely failed to sum up all that his ministry had meant to him and to those he served, and added, 'I trusted God, and I survived.'

His was a life of love and service, poured out for others, based on a profound trust in God, with beautiful effect. His ministry meant little in the grand scheme of the institutional church – he sat on no diocesan boards, took part in no public forums, held no positions of authority other than vicar, but he took seriously the 'pattern of his calling' as shepherd. He undertook no mass conversion rallies, but taught his congregation through his preaching. He gave no grand speeches, but said grace at harvest supper. He published no books but wrote faithfully each month in the parish magazine. He did indeed love his church communities, never failing to 'intercede on their behalf, and give thanks for them' (1 Timothy 2:1, NLT). The world may have been largely ignorant of his existence, but it was undoubtedly a better place for his having lived in it.

Writing from Macedonia sometime between AD61 and 63, the apostle Paul is instructing his fellow disciple Titus on how to complete his ministry in Crete before visiting Paul himself. The letter is for Titus' congregation as well as Titus himself, and it contains directions for appointing appropriate leaders, teaching sound doctrine and demonstrating how to live a Christian lifestyle. In these early verses, Paul is sharing the vital importance of sound leadership, recognising that the way a leader behaves – their motivation, words and actions – has a profound effect upon an entire community.

It may seem redundant for those of us reading this who are not bishops to learn what their qualities should be, but these qualities are for everyone in any position of authority – and there are few of us who exercise no authority over anyone. Being part of a family, a member of a club or engaged in charitable activities all involve elements of power and leadership, and those of us who aren't still demonstrate through our daily words and actions what it is to live as a believer, a follower of the Way.

We are to be 'God's stewards', faithfully caring not just for our fellow human beings but the whole of creation, responsible for its well-being and flourishing. We are to behave appropriately and to be 'trustworthy' in our grasp of the word. I suspect that, in this context, Paul is referring to the preaching and teaching tasks of the church leader, but I would like to expand this further. We should read and study our faith diligently, so that we continue to grow and mature in our knowledge and understanding. We should also 'grasp' the word more fully – living in it and through it, allowing the saving action of Jesus Christ to guide and influence every part of our lives. We should put our trust in this Word, completely and wholeheartedly.

Questions

- What should be the qualities of a leader? How might you encourage your church leader?

- How trustworthy are you as an example of Christian living? How might you become more trustworthy?

Prayer

> I thank Christ Jesus our Lord, who has given me strength, that he considered me trustworthy, appointing me to his service.
> 1 TIMOTHY 1:12 (NIV)

Thank you, Lord, that you have put your trust in me. Help me to put my trust in you as I live out your love. Amen

Wednesday 23 March

Reflecting

Psalm 22:1–8, 22–24

My God, my God, why have you forsaken me?
Why are you so far from helping me, from the words of my groaning?
O my God, I cry by day, but you do not answer;
and by night, but find no rest.
Yet you are holy,
enthroned on the praises of Israel.
In you our ancestors trusted;
they trusted, and you delivered them.
To you they cried, and were saved;
in you they trusted, and were not put to shame.
But I am a worm, and not human;
scorned by others, and despised by the people.
All who see me mock at me;
they make mouths at me, they shake their heads;
'Commit your cause to the Lord; let him deliver –
let him rescue the one in whom he delights!'...

I will tell of your name to my brothers and sisters;
in the midst of the congregation I will praise you:
You who fear the Lord, praise him!
All you offspring of Jacob, glorify him;
stand in awe of him, all you offspring of Israel!
For he did not despise or abhor
the affliction of the afflicted;
he did not hide his face from me,
but heard when I cried to him.

 Reflection

What a dark place the psalmist is in! And, sadly, I suspect it is a place that most, if not all of us, will recognise – for some it will be only too familiar. The feeling of isolation, of endless prayers, repeated night and day, which remain unanswered. The terrible fear that God is absent, if not from the entire world, then at least from us and our anguish. A pain and sorrow so terrible that we have become dehumanised in the experience – we are simply worms, creatures of sensation without any means of making sense of it all. I have a mental image of a human being all alone in a dark and stormy sea, head barely above the water, the bitter saltiness of the waves gradually overwhelming them while they cry out into the night.

Alone and stricken, the psalmist casts around for comfort. He remembers all the ways in which God has interceded for his people in the past. He remembers how their trust was not proved groundless but instead was validated by God's saving action. He clings on to a recitation of deliverance before being swept away by a feeling of worthlessness: 'All who see me mock at me.'

But the wave which threatened to sink him recedes as he remembers who it is who created him, who has kept him safe and whose purposes for him can only be good. He calls out now with more confidence, begging his creator, his last chance, to draw near.

And then, as a drowning man drops his feet one last time, having given up trying to keep afloat and resigned himself to sinking beneath the waves, one toe touches something solid. The toehold becomes a foothold, and the man realises he is standing on the solid ground of God's promise to each one of us that he will never forsake us. Beneath the seas of suffering is the rock of salvation, which thousands of years cannot wear away and which remains forever a support beneath our feet. Even amid the most terrible events, God is not absent – in fact, he has drawn nearer, offering comfort and support to those most in danger of submerging. Trusting in God, his rock and sure deliverer, the psalmist can turn his lament into praise. Even while the storm rages around him, he finds peace in his awareness of God's presence.

For us Christians, this psalm carries an extra resonance. Beginning with that famous cry, made by our Lord on the cross, moments before his saving mission for the world was completed, the thread of hope runs golden through this psalm. For Jesus Christ has taken on the experience of the psalmist and all for whom the beginning of this psalm is a familiar situation. He has lived through it, died in it and, in the dying, transformed and redeemed it. The cross is not just the punishment of one man but the suffering of humankind, willingly undergone in fulfilment of Old Testament prophecies, offered on behalf of all people for their salvation.

The resurrected Christ still bears the marks of the cross. For us, waiting in between times, living in a flawed and broken world and being flawed and broken ourselves, lament and praise must go hand in hand. We trust in the God who has already redeemed us, who has shown his care for us in the past and who continues to love us. We trust in the Son, who shares our suffering, bearing his wounds willingly for our sake. We trust in the Spirit, whose life-giving breath infuses every moment with hope, offering the certainty that this suffering will be redeemed and transformed. We are invited to call out to God in the darkness, to trust in his eternal and loving response and to praise him.

Questions

- In what ways do you resonate with this psalm? Have you been in a dark place or felt that God was absent?

- How do you remind yourself of God's presence?

Prayer

Heavenly Father, as we live in the space between this world and grace, help us to put our trust in your good purposes for us. Remind us of the ways in which you have worked in the past, and give us hope for the future, through the resurrection of Christ, our rock and deliverer. Amen

Thursday 24 March

Living

Isaiah 26:1–6

On that day this song will be sung in the land of Judah:

We have a strong city;
he sets up victory
like walls and bulwarks.
Open the gates,
so that the righteous nation that keeps faith
may enter in.
Those of steadfast mind you keep in peace –
in peace because they trust in you.
Trust in the Lord forever,
for in the Lord God
you have an everlasting rock.
For he has brought low
the inhabitants of the height;
the lofty city he lays low.
He lays it low to the ground,
casts it to the dust.
The foot tramples it,
the feet of the poor,
the steps of the needy.

Reflection

It is not the custom to write enthusiastically about building sites in books like this, but I have always been interested in them. When my children were young, we would spend a long time watching the diggers, tractors, cranes and bulldozers as they wove their complicated dance back and forth, sometimes working together, sometimes apart. Even now, with no small people as an excuse, I will stop and marvel at how gracefully the work is accomplished, giant machines and their diminutive drivers each occupied with their own task.

I have been watching one site recently which is located near my home, so that I drive past it fairly regularly. It began life as a green field on the outskirts of a small town, so it was startling to see one day that the field had been surrounded by tall grey fencing and that the bulldozers had moved in. In an instant, the grass disappeared and the meadow became a sea of mud, with yellow heavy machinery moving sturdily back and forth, operated by building contractors clad in equally bright yellow.

Everyone seemed so busy, and yet nothing seemed to be happening. For weeks, I waited for the first sign of brick walls to make their appearance, but still all was digging and concreting. Finally, the first courses of bricks made their appearance – and in no time at all, it seemed, I was watching the clean wooden roofing rafters being hammered in place and yellow-grey roofing tiles laid on top. I asked a friend of mine in the building trade whether this was normal, and he replied, 'It's all in the footings, you see. Get them right and the house goes up sweetly. Skimp on the footings and you are asking for disaster.'

Of course, as followers of Jesus we know all about the importance of building on firm foundations. The story of the wise man who built his house on the rock is likely to be familiar territory, as is the transference of that metaphor in Jesus' declaration of Peter as 'the rock':

> And I tell you, you are Peter, and on this rock I will build my church, and the gates of Hades will not prevail against it.
> MATTHEW 16:18

But the image of the rock, of the vital importance of sure foundations, reaches all through the Bible. As far back as Deuteronomy we have this declaration:

> For I will proclaim the name of the Lord;
> ascribe greatness to our God!
> The Rock, his work is perfect;
> and all his ways are just.
> A faithful God, without deceit,
> just and upright is he.
> DEUTERONOMY 32:3–4

And the references continue. Hannah's faith in God as her rock is rewarded with the birth of Samuel; David calls on God, his rock, whenever he is danger. By the time we reach the Psalms, the image of God as rock is settled in our imagination – and what a hugely powerful and reassuring image that is.

The writer of today's passage appears to begin his song mid-conversation. This is no carefully planned, premeditated deliberation, but an outpouring of praise and faith. The writer has been living in hope and faith, placing his trust in God as a natural part of his everyday life – what is written is simply what continues unspoken, merely the articulation of a lived emotion. Those who trust in God experience peace, because that trust is based on something so certain and true that nothing will destroy it. The writer can live free from fear, with no anxiety about the future, because he knows on what his future is built. Just as the inhabitant of the new houses, which I watched grow from soil to splendour, can rest secure in the knowledge that their homes will not collapse around them, so can we who build our lives on the rock of God's love rest in the knowledge that our lives will not collapse. Dwellings that have Christ as the cornerstone will last forever.

As children of God, heirs to the kingdom, our cities will be open to all who trust in him, and we will share our lives with our fellow citizens of faith:

> You are no longer strangers and aliens, but you are citizens with the saints and also members of the household of God, built upon the foundation of the apostles and prophets, with Christ Jesus himself as the cornerstone. In him the whole structure is joined together and grows into a holy temple in the Lord; in whom you also are built together spiritually into a dwelling-place for God.
> EPHESIANS 2:19–22

Questions

- What are the foundations of your life? What can you do to make them more secure?
- What does 'home' mean to you – consider the word in all its aspects. Do you have a 'home' in God?

Prayer

> *God is our fortress and our rock,*
> *our mighty help in danger;*
> *he shields us from the battle's shock*
> *and thwarts the devil's anger.*
> Martin Luther (1483–1546)

God, my rock, help me to build my life upon the certainty of your love for me. Help me to place all my trust in you. Give me the peace that flows from this trust so that I may live to praise your name. Amen

| Friday 25 March

Telling

Luke 18:9–14

[Jesus] also told this parable to some who trusted in themselves that they were righteous and regarded others with contempt: 'Two men went up to the temple to pray, one a Pharisee and the other a tax-collector. The Pharisee, standing by himself, was praying thus, "God, I thank you that I am not like other people: thieves, rogues, adulterers, or even like this tax-collector. I fast twice a week; I give a tenth of all my income." But the tax-collector, standing far off, would not even look up to heaven, but was beating his breast and saying, "God, be merciful to me, a sinner!" I tell you, this man went down to his home justified rather than the other; for all who exalt themselves will be humbled, but all who humble themselves will be exalted.'

Reflection

The 1995 Oscar-winning film *Braveheart* tells the story of William Wallace, who, with Robert the Bruce, led the Scottish rebellion against Edward I. The film opens with a panorama of the mountains and lochs of Scotland, and a voice declaring, 'I shall tell you of William Wallace. Historians from England will tell you I am a liar, but history is written by those who hanged heroes.' Although exaggerated in tone, this statement echoes a popular view of history – that it is written by the 'victors' – those who won the battles, those who succeeded in business, those who climbed the ladder of social status to reach the top.

It is the reason why we need to look at more than one source before we form an opinion – those who did less well financially or socially or those whose loved ones were killed in conflicts or who fled war zones might tell a different story. Only when we have listened to several different voices should we begin to form an opinion on the course of events and their outcome. This century has seen a rise in the number of different approaches to historical events – and the Bible has not proved immune to this. Stories have been rewritten from a woman's point of view or by studying the actions of the lesser characters – all to give a more rounded picture of the way God has worked in history, not only with the wealthy and powerful, but also with the poor and the outcast.

The least objective source of all, however, is often overlooked – how we ourselves are biased in our opinions and in how we interpret events and characters according to our own preconceptions and prejudices. A woman in one of the village churches made my life miserable. She complained endlessly about every detail, never hesitating to pick me up on any error I made. She frequently wrote letters pointing out my deficiencies and encouraged others to question even the least of my decisions. At her funeral, I was astonished as one after another of her friends and colleagues told how kind, patient and tolerant she was and how much fun and joy she brought into their lives. I could not believe it was the same person and returned home chastened as to my poor judgement of people.

The characters in today's reading have just such a problem with how they perceive people, only the people they misjudge are themselves. Jesus addresses a group of people who have two issues: first, they trust in themselves and their own excellence, and second, this attitude has led them to treat others 'with contempt'. Of course, it is important to have confidence in oneself – an element of self-belief is a vital part of living a secure and happy life. It is good to trust in ourselves and our ability to perform the tasks we are set; it is good to believe that one is essentially worthy. However, this self-belief should be tempered with self-awareness and humility. We are none of us perfect, and certainly none of us should rely on our own righteousness to keep us on the right track for eternal life.

The Pharisee seems to have it all going for him – in the words of the cliché, he is one of the 'victors' and has written his own history. In fact, it is not a prayer that he offers to God, but a paean of self-praise – the implication is that God is lucky to have him on board, so virtuous is he, so righteous.

The tax collector, however, knows his many faults, knows that it is by the grace of God alone that he dares to enter his presence to offer him praise and thanksgiving. 'All who humble themselves will be exalted,' says Jesus, reminding us that Christians must live in service to others, despising none but offering instead a life lived in a community of equality, all reliant on grace for their redemption. We should not, however, fall into the trap of self-deprecation, undervaluing the gifts that we have been given, despising ourselves for our lack of gifts. Instead, we should remember that we are all treasured by God and place our trust not in ourselves but in his love for us.

Questions

- Do you agree that 'history is written by the victors'? How would the Bible differ if it were written by women, for example?
- Do you have a realistic sense of your 'righteousness'? Do you trust in yourself too much or not enough? How might you alter the balance?

Prayer

With broken heart and contrite sigh,
a trembling sinner, Lord, I cry:
thy pardoning grace is rich and free,
O God, be merciful to me.
Cornelius Elven (1797–1873)

Heavenly Father, help me to place all my trust in you. Help me to believe in my own righteousness only so much as it is dependent upon your grace, for without you I am lost indeed. Amen

Saturday 26 March

Sharing

Revelation 21:1–6

Then I saw a new heaven and a new earth; for the first heaven and the first earth had passed away, and the sea was no more. And I saw the holy city, the new Jerusalem, coming down out of heaven from God, prepared as a bride adorned for her husband. And I heard a loud voice from the throne saying,

'See, the home of God is among mortals.
He will dwell with them;
they will be his peoples,
and God himself will be with them;
he will wipe every tear from their eyes.
Death will be no more;
mourning and crying and pain will be no more,
for the first things have passed away.'

And the one who was seated on the throne said, 'See, I am making all things new.' Also he said, 'Write this, for these words are trustworthy and true.' Then he said to me, 'It is done! I am the Alpha and the Omega, the beginning and the end. To the thirsty I will give water as a gift from the spring of the water of life.'

Reflection

One of my favourite films is *Seabiscuit* (2003). Set in the United States during the Great Depression, it charts the story of a racehorse, his owner, trainer and jockey, and the effect the horse has on not only their lives but also the mood of the nation. One of the most compelling scenes occurs early in the film. Seabiscuit's jockey confesses to the trainer that he is blind in one eye. The trainer, Tom, is furious and reports the matter to Seabiscuit's owner: 'He lied to us! You want a jockey who lies to us?' The owner thinks for a while, then replies, 'It's fine, Tom.' 'It's fine?' queries the trainer, astonished. 'It's fine. You don't throw a whole life away just because it's banged up a little.'

One of the reasons I love this passage from Revelation is that this same feeling is expressed here: 'And the one who was seated on the throne said, "See, I am making all things new."' God doesn't say, 'See, I am getting rid of all the old, damaged stuff. See, I am doing away with all the corrupted, rotten, out-of-date things. See, I will cleanse the world of sinful, ignorant, arrogant human beings. See, I will start again from the beginning.' Of course he doesn't. He promised us aeons ago that he would never again destroy the world:

> I have set my bow in the clouds, and it shall be a sign of the covenant between me and the earth. When I bring clouds over the earth and the bow is seen in the clouds, I will remember my covenant that is between me and you and every living creature of all flesh; and the waters shall never again become a flood to destroy all flesh.
>
> GENESIS 9:13–15

God doesn't throw our lives away just because they are banged up a little. He renews them!

And what's more, he will come down from heaven and dwell with us – the whole of creation will be renewed in the light of God's love. The words that God speaks here turn our expectations upside down. No longer do we look forward to a time when we will be transported off to some other plane of existence – God will meet us where we are and will renew and redeem who we are.

And because of Christ's life, death and resurrection, that renewal and redemption is happening now. Now, in the between times, we can still catch glimpses of the new Jerusalem which will descend from heaven, transforming all cities, all places where human beings live. Now, as we are held within the Alpha and the Omega, we are being shaped and formed by the indwelling of the Spirit. This new world will not be formed, or reformed, by God alone, but by his children working in partnership with him. We share with God the responsibility for renewal, not just in the work of catching glimpses of this new creation, but in actively striving to bring the kingdom into being.

The promises in this passage are immense. God will bring an end to 'mourning and crying and pain'. He has already defeated death. And we can hold fast to these promises because he tells us so: 'These words are trustworthy and true.' Trust me, God says, for I will not abandon you. Trust me, because I love you as one of my children. Trust my words, because I am your creator.

> Trust in the Lord with all your heart,
>   and do not rely on your own insight.
> In all your ways acknowledge him,
>   and he will make straight your paths.
>
> PROVERBS 3:5–6

Questions

- 'Learning to trust is one of life's most difficult tasks' (Isaac Watts, 1674–1748). Do you find it difficult or easy to trust other people? Who do you trust, and why?
- Do you find it difficult or easy to trust God?

Prayer

God of the new Jerusalem, help me to trust in you. Help me to imprint your words on my soul and allow them to make me new. Give me the strength to share in your task of building the new Jerusalem here where you will dwell with us. Amen

Sunday 27 March

Becoming

Matthew 25:14–19, 24–30 (CEV)

The kingdom is also like what happened when a man went away and put his three servants in charge of all he owned. The man knew what each servant could do. So he handed five thousand coins to the first servant, two thousand to the second, and one thousand to the third. Then he left the country.

As soon as the man had gone, the servant with the five thousand coins used them to earn five thousand more. The servant who had two thousand coins did the same with his money and earned two thousand more. But the servant with one thousand coins dug a hole and hid his master's money in the ground.

Some time later the master of those servants returned. He called them in and asked what they had done with his money…

The servant who had been given one thousand coins then came in and said, 'Sir, I know that you are hard to get along with. You harvest what you don't plant and gather crops where you haven't scattered seed. I was frightened and went out and hid your money in the ground. Here is every single coin!'

The master of the servant told him, 'You are lazy and good-for-nothing! You know that I harvest what I don't plant and gather crops where I haven't scattered seed. You could have at least put my money in the bank, so that I could have earned interest on it.'

Then the master said, 'Now your money will be taken away and given to the servant with ten thousand coins! Everyone

who has something will be given more, and they will have more than enough. But everything will be taken from those who don't have anything. You are a worthless servant, and you will be thrown out into the dark where people will cry and grit their teeth in pain.'

Reflection

One of the advantages of social media is that grandparents do not have to wait until they visit before they can witness the prodigious gifts of their grandchildren. Since becoming a granny, not a day has passed without me being sent a picture of a beloved grandchild's drawing or writing, a short film clip of a song or a dance, or simply a photo of a gappy smile as the first baby tooth falls out.

How tenderly we watch for signs of their gifts – 'She's going to be a footballer'; 'He will be a musician.' What efforts are made to encourage a particular skill or talent as parents patiently drive offspring to sports clubs and music school, swimming pools and dance studios. There comes a time, however, when the child decides for themselves in which direction they will go, and whether or not they will continue to put in the effort required to make the most of their gifts. At such a time, the parent can only step back and trust that lessons in perseverance and determination have not been in vain, and that their child will fulfil their potential in a way which brings them satisfaction – and hopefully enriches their community as well.

I always imagine the property owner in today's passage to be like this – to have encouraged and taught his employees so that they are now in a position to show how well they have learnt. The owner then steps back to give his people the space they need, demonstrating a trust in them and their abilities. Two of them vindicate the faith he has had in them, not only satisfying but exceeding his expectations. The third, however, fails to carry out his task, using his fear of the harshness of his employer as an excuse. This may be true or it may just be a way of hiding his laziness and lack of responsibility.

There is a danger in applying this parable to ourselves – we might see it as an exhortation to work harder, better and faster to gain the approval of a taskmaster God. But we know better than to assume that the way into the kingdom is through our own effort. As the apostle Paul wrote, 'But the people of Israel, who pursued the law as the way of righteousness, have not attained their goal. Why not? Because they pursued it not by faith but as if it were by works' (Romans 9:31–32, NIV). We are not judged on the quality or quantity of our achievements, but on how prepared we are to try. We are not asked to become world-famous explorers, surgeons or dancers. We are not even asked to become inspirational preachers or to convert hundreds to Christianity. All we are asked to do is to use what we have been given in the best way possible, to the glory of God and in the service of our fellow human beings. The third employee buried the money with which he was entrusted, thus abdicating all responsibility for it. It is for this he is judged, not for his failure to multiply what he was given.

Nor should we limit our interpretation of this parable simply to the gifts and skills with which we have been blessed. We should move beyond those things which the world values and even beyond the less obvious gifts – hospitality or kindness, service or generosity. This parable leads us to endeavour to do the best with everything that life gives us – even the things we don't want! Many of our problems are not our fault, but are thrust upon us by a broken world – the death of a spouse, illness, unemployment, loneliness, depression. Although not of our making, we should nonetheless take responsibility for them, not allowing them to warp or corrupt the way we see the world, refusing to give them the power to alter the way we behave towards others, using our experience perhaps to help others who face similar challenges.

And as with our gifts, we are not left to deal with our challenges on our own. We have our communities, our churches and the Holy Spirit, working with us and within us, encouraging us and enabling us to use all that we have been given in the service of our fellow human beings and to the glory of God.

Questions

- What are your gifts?
- What are your challenges?
- How might you use both to the glory of God?

Prayer

Come, labour on.
Cast off all gloomy doubt and faithless fear!
No arm so weak but may do service here.
Though feeble agents, may we all fulfil
God's righteous will.
Jane Borthwick (1813–97)

Holy Spirit, help me to step out boldly in the service of the kingdom. Help me to use all that I have been given for the benefit of others and in praise of God. Amen

Questions for group study

- Reflecting on this week's Bible passages, which ones have engaged you most? Which have you found most challenging? Has your understanding of trust changed and, if so, how?

- George Herbert, a priest and poet of the 17th century, writes in 'Affliction IV' of being 'a wonder tortur'd in the space betwixt this world and that of grace'. He then continues with the affirmation that God will transform the evil which besets him, 'with care and courage building me, till I reach heav'n, and much more, thee'. Do you find this picture of trust helpful?

- When have you prayed in trust? When have you prayed in desperation?

Creative prayer

Look back and remember: he was with you.
Stand still and realise: he is with you.
Walk forward and trust: he will be with you always.
Margaret Silf

Draw three hand shapes on three separate pieces of paper, and write one phrase on each hand. As you hold the first hand, remember all the times that God has been with you in the past, all the times when your trust in him has been validated.

Holding the second hand, think of all the ways in which God is supporting you now, the gifts he has given you in terms of relationships and experiences, and give thanks.

Finally, take the third hand and ask God for the grace to walk forward into your future, trusting in his good purpose for you.

Week 5 | Monday 28 March–Sunday 3 April

Sacrificing

One of the challenges of exploring 'sacrifice' is to rid ourselves of preconceived ideas of what the word means, so that we can come to the Bible with fresh eyes and an objective mind. For 'sacrifice' is a word laden with connotations – most of them bad.

Sadly, the story which the word brings quickest to mind is often that of Abraham and Isaac. I was tempted to shy away from that story, but instead I offer a number of ways of interpreting it and leave it to you to reflect upon.

God, however, desires 'mercy not sacrifice' – or rather, mercy as sacrifice, if we practise mercy in a truly selfless way, setting aside our own needs for those of others, putting down our grievances and the injustices offered to us so that we can offer forgiveness and peace to others. A sacrificial life is one which offers to God all the trials as well as the joys, all the challenges as well as the triumphs – accepting life in all its fullness and praising God throughout.

At the heart of this is the sacrifice of Christ on the cross, made once for all so that no further sacrifice is needed on our part in order to access forgiveness, love and eternal life.

Monday 28 March

Listening

Psalm 51:1–2, 12–17

Have mercy on me, O God,
 according to your steadfast love;
according to your abundant mercy
 blot out my transgressions.
Wash me thoroughly from my iniquity,
 and cleanse me from my sin…
Restore to me the joy of your salvation,
 and sustain in me a willing spirit.
Then I will teach transgressors your ways,
 and sinners will return to you.
Deliver me from bloodshed, O God,
 O God of my salvation,
 and my tongue will sing aloud of your deliverance.
O Lord, open my lips,
 and my mouth will declare your praise.
For you have no delight in sacrifice;
 if I were to give a burnt-offering, you would not be pleased.
The sacrifice acceptable to God is a broken spirit;
 a broken and contrite heart, O God, you will not despise.

Reflection

Like 'sacrifice', the word 'broken' is laden with negative connotations. The phrase 'broken bodies' brings to mind terrible images of pain and suffering – Christ on the cross; appalling road traffic accidents; battlefield injuries. Broken objects have lost their purpose – they can no longer be used or, if they still work, they either don't work as well or don't look as good as they did. Broken hearts are the saddest of all, implying an unhappy love affair, a trust betrayed or a disappointment so great that we no longer function as we once did. How can this be what God is looking for? Of what value to anyone is a broken spirit or a broken heart? Our God is one who mends, heals and redeems.

Perhaps we need to look at the word in a different way. A body that is broken knows the edge of its capabilities. It learns about vulnerability and frailty, and during the healing process it might learn dependence on others, a new level of humility and acceptance of personal limitations. Not for nothing does military training aim to drive each recruit to the point of exhaustion, of brokenness. It is only there that the true nature of a person's character can be established; it is only from a position of brokenness that something new can be built up.

Broken objects can be fixed in such a way that they look better than before. In the Japanese art of *kintsugi*, which is used in mending broken porcelain, the craftsperson doesn't try to conceal the fact that a valuable dish has been broken. Instead, the pieces are joined with lacquer mixed with molten gold, silver or platinum. The break is not disguised but becomes part of the history of the object – and the more valuable for that.

And what about our broken hearts? What about our experiences of loss and the damage done to us in our heart's core, making us no longer so optimistic, so trusting, so open to the world? How can God possibly want us to undergo these experiences in order to offer them to him? Perhaps the unbroken hearts are the proud ones, the prejudiced ones. Perhaps an unbroken heart is one which has not known suffering and therefore is less able to empathise with the suffering of others. Perhaps an unbroken heart is one which doesn't recognise its own failings and therefore cannot feel the subsequent remorse or contrition which is a necessary step towards full repentance and, in turn, complete forgiveness.

During training for ministry, students are encouraged to look at their prejudices and narrow-mindedness, their assumptions and selfishness. These are examined and laid bare, so that the shabbiness as well as the glory of the soul is seen. This process can seem like a breaking of one's personality, but it is rather a clearing of the worldly trains of thought which hide shoddy thinking and the removal of props which support an insubstantial faith. Once the external disguises have been removed, the heart, soul and mind can be rebuilt, formed and moulded after the pattern of Christ.

In today's psalm, David recognises that he has sinned, and he kneels before God in sorrow. He begs God to give him a 'clean heart' and a 'new and right spirit' (v. 10). It is only when he himself has been forgiven that he can lead others in the way of repentance. The sacrifice of a broken heart is a recognition before God of our own sin. It is the sacrifice of one who has examined their life and identified the times of selfishness and greed, arrogance and idleness. It is the bringing before God of all these times and asking in all humility for these offences to be taken away. Then we can sing aloud to God in praise. Then we can lead transgressors in God's ways. Then we can truly dance before the Lord.

Questions

- What do you think is a 'broken heart'? Has your heart ever been broken? How did the experience change you?
- How might your experience enable you to come closer to God, and to help others?

Prayer

Then will I teach the world thy ways;
sinners shall learn thy sov'reign grace;
I'll lead them to my Savior's blood,
and they shall praise a pard'ning God.
Isaac Watts (1674–1748)

Forgiving God, help me to look inside my heart and see the brokenness. Heal those parts which prevent me from walking in your paths, and help me to share that healing with those I encounter on the way. Amen

Tuesday 29 March

Understanding

Matthew 9:9–13

As Jesus was walking along, he saw a man called Matthew sitting at the tax booth; and he said to him, 'Follow me.' And he got up and followed him.

And as he sat at dinner in the house, many tax-collectors and sinners came and were sitting with him and his disciples. When the Pharisees saw this, they said to his disciples, 'Why does your teacher eat with tax-collectors and sinners?' But when he heard this, he said, 'Those who are well have no need of a physician, but those who are sick. Go and learn what this means, "I desire mercy, not sacrifice." For I have come to call not the righteous but sinners.'

Reflection

There are many advantages to being a child of the vicarage, rectory, manse or whatever your denomination calls it. A lot of people know who you are and stop to talk to you, which makes you feel significant. Your house is usually large and equipped to a good standard, if a bit chilly at times because heating is so expensive. You learn about serving others from a very early age and have the benefits of being a member of a community.

However, the drawbacks are also many – you may never feel truly 'at home', as you might move house often and the house isn't yours anyway. Opportunities for anonymity are limited, and people feel free to comment on your behaviour and upbringing. You are dragged in to help with nativity plays, readings, serving coffee and moving chairs and you must at all times be polite, however rude someone is to you.

As part of the first batch of women with children working as Anglican priests, I was forging a new and often challenging path of combining ministry with motherhood, and my children have many tales of their experiences as 'vicarage children' – and some scars as well. One of the most useful pieces of advice I was given as a curate was from a vicar nearing retirement who warned me in a low and serious tone to 'never sacrifice your children on the altar of your ministry'. I took that to mean that I should protect family time, prioritise school events and try not to bring my work home with me in terms of distressing tales or experiences. I have tried to honour that – with more or less success.

It is easy to slip into focusing on what we must do to earn God's favour, what sacrifices we must make in order to truly follow Christ: attend church regularly; study the Bible; pray regularly; avoid overindulging in food or drink; serve our neighbours; put others' wishes before our own. All these things are righteous, and they can all be life-enhancing. But if we are undertaking them solely so that we can prove ourselves worthy of God's love, we are doing them with the wrong motive.

It is easier still to sacrifice others – excluding them if they do not agree with our way of worship; distancing ourselves from those with whom we disagree instead of engaging with them in order to understand their point of view; passing by the hurting, the disturbed and the unfortunate because they don't fit in with our world view.

Jesus calls us to be merciful to ourselves and to others – to behave with compassion and forgiveness, tolerance and respect. Showing mercy to ourselves involves not pushing ourselves to breaking point, not allowing ourselves to become broken by obligation and duty, and forgiving ourselves when we do not live up to the high standards we have set ourselves – the high standards we feel we need to attain if we are to be truly loved by God. Showing mercy to ourselves means relaxing into God's love for us, acknowledging that we do not have to earn grace, because it has already been freely offered to us, and rejoicing in our status as children of God.

Showing mercy to others means listening to those around us, sharing in their lives and including them in ours, encouraging and supporting them, and welcoming them in the name of Jesus, the bringer of healing and love. Seen in this way, mercy has elements of sacrifice about it – the careful awareness of the needs of others as well as respect for our own tender service to those with whom we share our lives; the recognition of the importance of times of rest and relaxation for ourselves.

Followers of the Way do not need to make sacrifices in order to win God's favour – the death and resurrection of Christ has opened up the path of righteousness to all who choose to walk in it. But we do need to show mercy to ourselves and others as we journey together, rejoicing in his love. And we should remember that always there is something new to learn – about mercy as well as sacrifice.

Questions

- Have there been times when you have sacrificed yourself for others?
- Have there been times when you have sacrificed others? How did that make you feel? Looking back, was there another way?

Prayer

Lord Jesus, as we hear your call to follow you, help us to acknowledge that, sinful as we are, we cannot hope to earn your love. Help us to rejoice that the love we desire is given to us freely, so that we might live joyful lives, trusting in you. Teach us merciful living, and help us to show mercy to ourselves and to others, in your name. Amen

Wednesday 30 March

Reflecting

Genesis 4:1–7

> Now the man knew his wife Eve, and she conceived and bore Cain, saying, 'I have produced a man with the help of the Lord.' Next she bore his brother Abel. Now Abel was a keeper of sheep, and Cain a tiller of the ground. In the course of time Cain brought to the Lord an offering of the fruit of the ground, and Abel for his part brought of the firstlings of his flock, their fat portions. And the Lord had regard for Abel and his offering, but for Cain and his offering he had no regard. So Cain was very angry, and his countenance fell. The Lord said to Cain, 'Why are you angry, and why has your countenance fallen? If you do well, will you not be accepted? And if you do not do well, sin is lurking at the door; its desire is for you, but you must master it.'

Reflection

This is a tale of two churches. Both were small, ancient buildings, each with their fair share of dilapidation and challenges. Neither had a large number of worshippers, as the population of their villages was small and elderly. However, the communities were generally prosperous – employment was high, the schools were good and the nearby town was large enough to meet some desires as well as most needs. Each church was the only public building in the community, the only place where everyone could gather on equal terms, owing no one the obligations of host or guest.

In one church there had developed the culture of careful accounting. Aware that money was short, every effort was made to save it. The heating was rarely turned on, service booklets were allowed to grow tatty and the altar linen was faded and much darned. The congregation had got into the habit of using the church to deposit cast-off furniture and other goods – things that still had some life in them but were too old, too shabby or too knocked about to be welcome in their homes. By and by the church began to look shabby and knocked about as well. Fewer people came, and those who did grumbled about the cold, the missing pages from the tatty hymnbooks and the trip hazards caused by worn carpeting and curled-up rugs. The worship was correspondingly lacklustre, as people huddled together for warmth and merely wished the service to be over soon so that they could return home.

In contrast, the neighbouring church adopted a strategy of cheerful giving. A conscious decision was made that the church should be a place of excellence, as far as possible. Donors were sought for new carpets, skilled needleworkers embroidered new altar linen and the local printer was negotiated with to produce new booklets. The heating was switched on well before the service began and a collection of cheerful blankets was offered at the entrance of the church to those who might still feel the chill of the ancient building in their bones. The congregation grew in numbers. People felt the warmth of human welcome and appreciated the efforts made to maximise all that the building could offer. As the building was valued and considered worthy of sacrifice, so too were the people who visited it. This had the effect of building up the sense of community and encouraging giving in turn. The worship was lively and engaging, and friendships were formed and spilled over into increased involvement in other village activities.

This sounds like a fairy story – particularly the part where the church congregation grows. But I have witnessed this not just once but many times, and it all begins with an attitude, a conscious decision about the place of 'church' in the life of a person and a community. Will it come at the top of people's lists or the bottom? Will it have a priority or merely an insignificant place among all the other obligations?

The well-known story of Cain and Abel, and the choices they make, is the first example in the Bible of the importance of attitude. Things have moved on since Adam and Eve were expelled from the garden of Eden. Years of hard work have been put in, with visible results – there are now crops to be cultivated and flocks to be herded. Adam and Eve have sons, and these sons are put in charge of ensuring the family has enough food. No doubt they work hard at this and spend hours labouring at their respective tasks.

The time comes to give back to God a part of all that he has given them in terms of water, sunshine, fertile soil and their own health and strength. Abel considers carefully what he should give; he chooses the 'firstlings', the best of all he has. Cain, however, has a different attitude. Perhaps he resents giving even a small part of what he has worked so hard to obtain; perhaps he thinks that anything will do.

But there is a reckoning – Abel's sacrifice is accepted, and Cain's is not. God has seen the attitude behind the gift and admonishes Cain. But even then Cain cannot accept that he has given grudgingly and sparingly. 'Sin is lurking at the door,' warns God – this lack of generosity opens the path to a more generalised selfishness; Cain's attitude of putting himself before anyone leads to hardness of heart and carelessness of others – and thus a murderer is made.

Questions

- What is the attitude of your worshipping community? Is it open and generous or closed and tight?
- Is your building filled with the best you can provide or cast-offs? How might you change this?

Prayer

Gracious God, give us a generous spirit so that we may worship you joyfully and wholeheartedly. Let our 'sacrifice of thanks and praise' be genuine and heartfelt. Give us the grace to avoid the temptations of selfishness and help us to close the door against all sin. Amen

Thursday 31 March

Living

Genesis 22:1–3, 9–14

After these things God tested Abraham. He said to him, 'Abraham!' And he said, 'Here I am.' He said, 'Take your son, your only son Isaac, whom you love, and go to the land of Moriah, and offer him there as a burnt-offering on one of the mountains that I shall show you.' So Abraham rose early in the morning, saddled his donkey, and took two of his young men with him, and his son Isaac; he cut the wood for the burnt-offering, and set out and went to the place in the distance that God had shown him...

When they came to the place that God had shown him, Abraham built an altar there and laid the wood in order. He bound his son Isaac, and laid him on the altar, on top of the wood. Then Abraham reached out his hand and took the knife to kill his son. But the angel of the Lord called to him from heaven, and said, 'Abraham, Abraham!' And he said, 'Here I am.' He said, 'Do not lay your hand on the boy or do anything to him; for now I know that you fear God, since you have not withheld your son, your only son, from me.' And Abraham looked up and saw a ram, caught in a thicket by its horns. Abraham went and took the ram and offered it up as a burnt-offering instead of his son. So Abraham called that place 'The Lord will provide'; as it is said to this day, 'On the mount of the Lord it shall be provided.'

 Reflection

I have to admit I very nearly changed my mind about including this reading. It was part of the original proposal, but when it actually came to reflecting and writing I found myself in a real fix. I have read many commentaries on the story of Abraham and Isaac, and I have reflected long and hard – but still I am undecided as to the meaning of the event and its place in the Christian story. So all I can do is set before you some different viewpoints, and let you reflect and choose.

It could be that this is a barbaric tale from an ancient time, one that explains the move from human sacrifice to that of animals. It might simply be an account of horrific child abuse, where a man is willing to murder his child, using the defence 'I was only obeying orders' – an excuse later used at the trials of Nazi concentration camp officials.

It could be that Abraham fails in his task. It could be that God is testing Abraham to see whether he will put his sacred duty as parent before his obligation to God – and Abraham doesn't do that. Abraham is prepared to sacrifice Isaac to his ambitions, for the sake of his position as God's favoured one.

On the other hand, it could be that this is a marvellous example of great faith – a faith against all odds, a foreshadowing of God's own sacrifice of his own Son so that all might live. In the covenant God made with Abraham, God promised that Abraham would be the father of multitudes, and that this would come about through Isaac. Isaac is the physical manifestation of the covenant – what will happen if that is removed? Does Abraham believe that God can carry out his promise if the apparent means of doing so are absent?

It could be that God is testing Abraham to the ultimate point, because God is risking the salvation of the world on Abraham, and he wants to be sure that Abraham is up to the task. After all, Abraham has previously not done so well at some things – pretending Sarah was his sister; sleeping with Hagar and subsequently sending her and their son Ishmael into the desert; refusing to believe in the angels' promise that Abraham and Sarah would have a son together. A man who is carrying the future of the nations needs to have rock-solid faith, needs to be supremely obedient so that the purposes of God can be carried out through him.

It could be that God is reminding Abraham – and us – that everything we have and are is a gift from him. We own nothing ourselves; we come into the world empty-handed and leave it the same way. Our task is not to have too tight a grip on our possessions and relationships, whether material or emotional, objects or human beings, that we cannot see past them to the divine giver. The person who can let go of the most precious thing in their life in obedience to the one who gave them that gift has great faith indeed. Abraham worked out his salvation in 'fear and trembling', just as 'God is working in you to make you willing and able to obey him' (Philippians 2:12–13, CEV).

I have thought and prayed about this passage, but I still fail to understand it or to appreciate what Abraham did. I have two sons and I cannot imagine killing them. If to do so were a test, I would fail it completely. But I also know that whatever my failings, and there are many, I have a God who did not draw back from sacrifice, and because of this sacrifice, I and my sons will live.

Question

- Pray and reflect on this passage – what does it mean to you?

Prayer

Lord Jesus Christ, Son of God, I have no words to pray. I have faith, but not enough; I have love, but my love is a poor, feeble thing; I have hope, but even this leaves me at times. But your sacrifice for me means that my faith, love and hope, insufficient as they are, are made sufficient in you, and for that I praise you. Amen

Friday 1 April

Telling

1 Corinthians 5:6–8 (KJV)

Your glorying is not good. Do you not know that a little leaven leavens the whole lump? Therefore purge out the old leaven, that you may be a new lump, since you truly are unleavened. For indeed Christ, our Passover, was sacrificed for us. Therefore let us keep the feast, not with old leaven, nor with the leaven of malice and wickedness, but with the unleavened bread of sincerity and truth.

Reflection

This is one of the few passages where not only do we have to understand something of New Testament cooking practices, but we also have to take care to use the correct Bible translation. The New King James Version here uses the word 'leaven' to indicate what other translations call 'yeast'. There is a world of difference. In New Testament times, bread was made by keeping back a small amount of dough from the last batch. It would be put aside for a few days and, in the warmth of the Middle Eastern climate, would begin to ferment. Once this process had happened, the fermented dough was then used as a raising agent – a leaven – for the next batch of bread, with a small amount once again being put aside so the process could continue.

As time went on, this leaven would become more infected with the bacteria and dirt from ordinary living, and each time another batch of bread was made, this dirt was incorporated into it. Therefore, unlike yeast, leaven was not necessarily a good thing but could carry its infections on and on until a clean break was made. Once a year, at the Feast of the Passover, the Jewish people were commanded to eat unleavened bread. All the leaven was cleaned from the house, and not until after the festival would a new batch of leaven be started.

The metaphor Paul is using in this passage now becomes clearer. Immediately preceding this passage, Paul has been admonishing the Corinthians for their failure to deal with sexual immorality within their church community. His instructions include cleansing not only the community from sin, but individuals as well. Paul is beseeching the members of the church in Corinth to take care to clear out all sin from their community and themselves. Every scrap has to go. Just as even a little leaven will pollute the whole dough, just one person can corrupt a community; even the slightest sin will contaminate the soul. He goes on to remind his listeners that it is vital to cleanse out the leaven, because each one of them is already unleavened! Through the sacrifice of Christ, the sins of believers have been thoroughly cleansed – all that remains is to make that fact a reality.

Many Bible commentators translate this complicated theology simply as 'become as you are'. This is a wonderfully affirming instruction – it acknowledges the fact that we are both fully redeemed in Christ and still have a bit of work to do.

I am reminded of when my children were teenagers and returned home 'hangry' after a long day at school. The term 'hangry' is a combination of 'hungry' and 'angry' and refers to being irrationally and unreasonably annoyed not because of any actual event but simply from lack of food. It is quickly remedied with large quantities of toast and jam. I became used to keeping silent until after the hangry teenager had eaten, trusting that once this had happened they would return to being their normal, lovely selves.

In the same way, God can see through the cloak of our selfish, greedy, lazy, hateful actions to the unique, wonderful soul which each one of us possesses. We cannot 'unleaven' ourselves – we do not need to, that task has been accomplished for us through the sacrifice of Christ. But we can try to adopt holy habits, maintaining our relationship with God through prayer and with our neighbours through service, helping those who are more vulnerable than we are, offering hospitality to all and working to build a community of faith and joy. Christ makes us new and uncorrupted. We must follow our calling to become who we are.

 Questions

- What sort of 'leaven' is left in your soul? What are the unhealthy habits which you still cling to? How might you cleanse yourself?
- Paul tells us to celebrate the feast with 'sincerity and truth' – how might this be put into practice with regards to yourself as an individual and as a member of your worshipping community?

 Prayer

Thank you, Lord Jesus Christ, for the sacrifice you have made for me. Because of your action, I am redeemed. I ask you now for the gift of grace so that I may become what I already am, and celebrate your feast with joy and thanksgiving. Amen

Saturday 2 April

Sharing

Mark 12:28–34

One of the scribes came near and heard them disputing with one another, and seeing that [Jesus] answered them well, he asked him, 'Which commandment is the first of all?' Jesus answered, 'The first is, "Hear, O Israel: the Lord our God, the Lord is one; you shall love the Lord your God with all your heart, and with all your soul, and with all your mind, and with all your strength." The second is this, "You shall love your neighbour as yourself." There is no other commandment greater than these.' Then the scribe said to him, 'You are right, Teacher; you have truly said that "he is one, and besides him there is no other"; and "to love him with all the heart, and with all the understanding, and with all the strength", and "to love one's neighbour as oneself", – this is much more important than all whole burnt-offerings and sacrifices.' When Jesus saw that he answered wisely, he said to him, 'You are not far from the kingdom of God.' After that no one dared to ask him any question.

Reflection

Sin offerings at the temple were a reminder that sin is a terrible thing, and that it must be atoned for with blood. Worshippers in Jesus' time were obedient to the age-old system of animal sacrifice as atonement for their sins. Live animals were taken and killed as an act of repentance. The animal could be an ox, a cow, a sheep or a goat, with doves or pigeons for those who could not afford a larger animal. There was a set ritual with prescribed steps and actions, and the animal was slaughtered and then burnt.

Other offerings could also be made. Baked flour, grain, oil and salt, accompanied by wine, was offered in grateful thanks for God's good provision, as was the peace offering – a sacrifice of an unblemished animal and grain made in thanksgiving and fellowship.

These were all straightforward, with clear-cut steps and equally clear consequences – atonement for sin, thanksgiving, worship and fellowship. These were the bedrock of Jewish worship.

But then Jesus arrived, overturning everything as usual. Loving God is the most important thing to do, with loving your neighbour a close second. These two things are more important than any kind of offering or sacrifice, however generous they are, in whatever spirit they are offered. This was not easy news. Why would anyone want to cast aside a ritual practice which has been in place for hundreds of years? More particularly, why would anyone want to swap a simple transaction of offering and atonement for the vastly more complex task of loving God and one's neighbour?

Because it isn't easy to love God all the time, is it? It's fine when things are going well for us – when we got the job we wanted or our house move went well. It's easy to offer praise and thanksgiving when we meet our life partner, when our children are born healthy and whole, when our finances are in the black. But what about in the tough times? How easy is it to be thankful when we are made redundant, we fall sick or someone we love dies?

When peace like a river, attendeth my way,
when sorrows like sea billows roll;
whatever my lot, Thou hast taught me to know
it is well, it is well, with my soul.

Thus wrote Horatio Spafford in 1873, having witnessed, in just four years, the death of his son, the collapse of his business enterprise and the drowning of all four of his daughters. What a triumph of faith – but one which few of us might be equal to.

And what about loving our neighbour? Once again, this is easy to do when our neighbour chats in a friendly manner over the fence, lends us their power tools or bakes us a cake. It is not so easy when we are in conflict over property boundaries, disagree over church strategy or are arguing about public amenities. It is not so easy when their loud laugh irritates us or their music keeps us awake.

And still we continue, our daily lives a constant sacrifice of love and praise, offering all the irritations as well as all the joys, all the struggles as well as all the triumphs, all the sorrows as well as all the happiness, which makes up who we are and what we do. And in it all, alongside us, encouraging us, supporting us, is Christ, who by his own sacrifice makes ours perfect.

Because we no longer have to make a sin offering. We no longer have to make burnt sacrifices in atonement for all the wrong we have done and the hurt we have caused. Christ's death has put us right with God, once and for all, and our sacrifices are changed. No longer made in a spirit of fear, but in rejoicing; no longer in exchange for something, but offered freely, as that which was offered to us was freely given, as we draw ever nearer to the kingdom of God.

Though Satan should buffet, though trials should come,
let this blest assurance control,
that Christ has regarded my helpless estate,
and hath shed His own blood for my soul.

My sin, oh, the bliss of this glorious thought!
My sin, not in part but the whole,
is nailed to the cross, and I bear it no more.
Praise the Lord, praise the Lord, O my soul!
Horatio Spafford (1828–88)

Questions

- Which is more challenging for you – to love God or to love your neighbour?

- How might you do either better?

Prayer

Heavenly Father, thank you that the sacrifice of your Son accomplished all that sacrifice can. Thank you that his offering of himself atoned for all my sins. Help me in my daily offering of love for you and for my neighbour so that I may draw ever nearer to you. Amen

Sunday 3 April

Becoming

Romans 12:1–2

I appeal to you therefore, brothers and sisters, by the mercies of God, to present your bodies as a living sacrifice, holy and acceptable to God, which is your spiritual worship. Do not be conformed to this world, but be transformed by the renewing of your minds, so that you may discern what is the will of God – what is good and acceptable and perfect.

Reflection

The contemporary Anglican marriage service is beautifully crafted. This is not surprising, as it is based on the 400-year-old Book of Common Prayer service and has been updated by a group of committed and inspired theologians. The service reminds me of a game of pass the parcel, where the prize is wrapped in layers of paper, each containing a smaller gift. The outer layers of the parcel are the entrance of the bride and the exit of the married couple. These are the party layers, the glamorous frothy sections where we celebrate and rejoice. As we go further in, the layers become more serious – there is the declaration by bride and groom that there are no legal barriers to their marriage and the signing of the registers. This declares to the world that their status has changed – from now on, they are each other's next of kin.

But all this pales into insignificance beside the central point of the service – the point where witnesses are no longer necessary, the world is excluded and even the minister's part is simply that of facilitator. Two people stand before God and make vows to each other which are solemnly binding and all-encompassing. In beautiful words, the bride and groom give themselves completely to each other – body, heart and mind. 'With my body I honour you, all that I am I give to you, and all that I have I share with you.' It is only after those words have been spoken that the minister declares the couple are husband and wife. From then on, each must put the other first, each must share with the other, each must live for and with the other.

This, for me, is the example that springs to mind when I read today's passage. The apostle Paul is reminding us of the gifts we have been given, of the many great causes for thanksgiving that each of us possess. Everything we have and are is through the mercy of God, and for that alone we offer thanks and praise. But our offering is not to be merely that of some part of our finances or some section of our day given up to voluntary work. It is not even joining with others in worship, studying the Bible or offering up prayers and intercessions on behalf of the world. We are to offer our bodies, hearts, minds and souls up to God, completely and utterly – everything that we have and everything that we are. We are to become a 'living sacrifice'.

This is not to be done on a transactional basis – we do not make an offering so that we might in return be gifted with something we value. Everything we need has already been given to us through the complete and eternal sacrifice of Christ. What we offer is done by grace with thanksgiving. We allow the Spirit of thanksgiving to transform us, constantly seeking to live in the light and love of Christ, allowing him to renew our minds daily so that we may be more closely aligned to his good purposes for us and for the whole world.

But the living sacrifice we are beseeched to become is not an individual act; it is a corporate one. Paul asks us to present our 'bodies' as one 'living sacrifice', reminding us once again that we do not act alone but as members of the body of Christ, the church:

> For just as each of us has one body with many members, and these members do not all have the same function, so in Christ we, though many, form one body, and each member belongs to all the others. We have different gifts, according to the grace given to each of us.
>
> ROMANS 12:4–6 (NIV)

Each of us has something to offer. Each of us has gifts to share, gifts given to us by God, to be used by us to his glory. So we bring to mind that wonderful wedding image in Revelation, where we witness the transformation of the whole world, as the 'Holy City, the new Jerusalem' descends 'as a bride beautifully dressed for her husband' (Revelation 21:2, NIV).

Paul's letter to the Romans continues by showing us what it looks like when everyone presents themselves as a living sacrifice:

> Be devoted to one another in love. Honour one another above yourselves. Never be lacking in zeal, but keep your spiritual fervour, serving the Lord. Be joyful in hope, patient in affliction, faithful in prayer. Share with the Lord's people who are in need. Practise hospitality.
>
> ROMANS 12:10–13 (NIV)

And all this begins with an openness to God's will, a readiness to be vulnerable for the sake of others and a joyful attitude of love and service.

Questions

- What do you think it means to be a living sacrifice? Do you feel you are being one at the moment?
- How might you offer your life to God and your neighbour in a way that is meaningful?

Prayer

Lord God, renew my mind so that I too might discern your will and live according to your purposes for me. Help me to offer my life for you in praise and thanksgiving, mindful always of your love and grace. Amen

Questions for group study

- Reflecting on this week's Bible passages, which ones have engaged you most? Which have you found most challenging? Has your understanding of sacrifice changed and, if so, how?

- What do you think of the idea that 'mercy is sacrifice'?

- What for you is 'a sacrifice of praise with thanksgiving'? What does it entail?

Creative prayer

You will need some beads and something to thread them on to. You can buy beads online or buy some necklaces from a charity shop, take them apart and keep the beads you like.

Put the beads in a bowl, and hold the thread, knotted at one end. As you thread each bead, thank God for a blessing in your life. This could be a person, an event or a situation. Once you have finished, tie off the thread. Keep the beads by you as a reminder or put them in your prayer space.

Week 6 | Monday 4 April–Sunday 10 April

Loving

We have arrived at Passion Week – the week before Holy Week – and the subject of love. This is possibly the most challenging of all, both to understand and to practise. We are asked to be perfect in our love – to extend our love to those most unworthy in our eyes, most undeserving, most difficult and demanding. We are asked to love without ceasing and to love without counting the cost, regardless of where this takes us or what effort it requires.

But in return we are promised the companionship of Christ, an engagement with all that is best and most precious and most profound in the world, a glimpse of the kingdom and an opportunity to partake in that kingdom by sharing it with others.

Monday 4 April

Listening

Matthew 5:43–48

You have heard that it was said, 'You shall love your neighbour and hate your enemy.' But I say to you, Love your enemies and pray for those who persecute you, so that you may be children of your Father in heaven; for he makes his sun rise on the evil and on the good, and sends rain on the righteous and on the unrighteous. For if you love those who love you, what reward do you have? Do not even the tax-collectors do the same? And if you greet only your brothers and sisters, what more are you doing than others? Do not even the Gentiles do the same? Be perfect, therefore, as your heavenly Father is perfect.

Reflection

I was recently talking to the mother of a six-year-old boy, and she was anxious about her son's failure to grasp the basics of reading, especially the fact that he wouldn't even try. He is a bright, clever boy, with all the advantages of a stable, happy life with plenty of access to learning material and support. But put him in front of a book and he was a different child, and this was affecting the rest of his behaviour as well. 'The trouble is,' said his mother, 'he wants to be good at it already. He cannot bear not being able to read, so he doesn't want to try.'

A teacher friend of mine joined the conversation and suggested that the mother make learning to read into a game rather than a task – words pinned on objects at home; instructions for favourite computer games to be read rather than listened to; word games played at home. After a few weeks of this, the barrier had been broken. The boy had begun to realise how key the skill of reading was, and how much information could be unlocked with it. He began to enjoy the struggle of learning new words and the feeling of triumph at successfully completing a reading book. This success overflowed into other areas of his life, and he became once more the sunny-tempered boy he had been before he ever encountered a reading scheme.

'Be perfect,' Jesus tells us. 'Go right ahead – achieve that! You must be just like me.' How our hearts quail at the thought. We who have gained years of life experience know that perfection always lies just out of reach. However hard we try, however many hours of practice we put in, we will not achieve perfection – not in anything.

Even worse, this perfection we are told to achieve is not in something concrete or measurable, such as the perfect sponge cake, the perfect wood carving or the perfect music performance. Rather, it is in the practice of love! How do we force ourselves to love people who are essentially, or so it seems to us, unlovable? Surely that falls into the trap of faith through works, where we diligently try to earn ourselves a place in the kingdom by sheer effort of will? Or should we just admit that we will never be perfect, so actually there is little point in trying – far easier to sit back and wait for God's grace to fill in the gaps and do all the hard work. We are only human, after all.

But there's the problem. Because through becoming human himself, Jesus taught us what true humanity looks like – and it involves love. Lots of love, the type of love which drives out darkness and hate, which brings in light, hope and a peace-filled future. Jesus isn't commanding us to perfection, so much as promising it to us. We will indeed be perfect once we stop dividing the world into people we love and people we don't need to love. We will be perfect when we accept that, just as the sun shines on all people indiscriminately, so the way to the kingdom is lit with love for everyone. Jesus looks at each one of us and sees in us all that we are able to become and how each one of us can change our own part of the world through the simple act of loving.

But this work of love is demanding. Jesus' instructions are fierce and uncompromising – if we are struck, we are not to strike back; if we are robbed, we are not to take anything away in retaliation. This is not a vague, 'I love everyone in the world', fluffy, indiscriminate love. This is the work of loving the neighbour who regularly parks across our drive, the group of teenagers playing on the children's swings, the community member who is argumentative and combative and the person who never does their fair share but criticises whatever anyone else does. This is the work of inviting people into our home, sacrificing our time and money in a good cause and constantly giving without expecting anything in return.

We will not bring in the kingdom through our efforts – that is God's work. But we will begin to live in a way that allows its entry into the world.

Questions

- 'Darkness cannot drive out darkness – only light can do that. Hate cannot drive out hate – only love can do that' (Martin Luther King, Jr, 1929–68). How can you drive out darkness and hate from your community?
- What expression of love are you going to articulate today?

Prayer

If we pray for those we do not love, we may or may not change them – that is up to God. What is certain is that we will change ourselves. Pray today for the gift of love and the opportunity to practise it. Amen

| Tuesday 5 April

Understanding

Mark 10:17–22

As [Jesus] was setting out on a journey, a man ran up and knelt before him, and asked him, 'Good Teacher, what must I do to inherit eternal life?' Jesus said to him, 'Why do you call me good? No one is good but God alone. You know the commandments: "You shall not murder; You shall not commit adultery; You shall not steal; You shall not bear false witness; You shall not defraud; Honour your father and mother."' He said to him, 'Teacher, I have kept all these since my youth.' Jesus, looking at him, loved him and said, 'You lack one thing; go, sell what you own, and give the money to the poor, and you will have treasure in heaven; then come, follow me.' When he heard this, he was shocked and went away grieving, for he had many possessions.

Reflection

Archbishop of York Stephen Cottrell wrote of his stock response to those asking for spiritual direction from him: 'Please make sure you bring your credit card statement with you.' This rather alarming instruction springs from the belief that the way we spend our money reflects those things we hold of greatest importance. This is an interesting approach to spirituality, and one which Jesus was clearly sharing when he told the rich young man to go away and give all he had to the poor, before following him.

Jesus had spotted that, despite the young man's earnest desire to gain access to the kingdom, his entire mindset was wrong. Once again we meet a character who is trapped in the transactional approach to the kingdom of heaven: 'What must I do?' he asks. What actions must I undertake, what rules must I follow, what exchange must I enter into before I can achieve my goal? Yet even this apparent willingness to undergo all sorts of trials and overcome all obstacles is limited – and Jesus identifies this immediately. The young man is only prepared to do what can be done easily, only prepared to sacrifice that for which he has no great care. When it comes to the things that are closest to his heart, he cannot bring himself to cut loose all that binds him to earthly values in order to become truly free.

And we are the same, aren't we? For some of us, our lack of generosity springs from a deep-seated fear of poverty, perhaps going back as far as childhood shortages. For others, our greed for material possessions or simply our delight in accumulating and collecting will be instrumental in preventing us from giving all that we should to those in need. 'How much is enough?' is a question that should always be at the top of our minds as we consider how enslaved we are by material goods and how much this impacts our spiritual well-being.

For others, there might well be no problem with giving away money or worldly possessions – we may be totally at ease with a lack of material goods, happy simply to have the basics rather than indulge in the luxuries which we are encouraged to purchase by the torrent of advertising which is daily directed at us. But even the materially generous might have difficulty in giving away other things – they might cling too closely to whatever power and authority is theirs, preferring perhaps to gain and keep control over people and situations rather than encourage and enable others to use their gifts of leadership. Perhaps the ability to give love and affection has been damaged by past experience, and relationships are problematic and self-seeking as friendship becomes a one-way street, with affirmation and love doled out in meagre quantities. This applies also to church communities – are we generous in our giving to other communities or do we keep all that we have to ourselves, in fear of worse times to come, perhaps, or convincing ourselves that we alone know how best to spend what we have?

For all but the most saintly few, there will be obstacles which lie in the way of our following Jesus with our whole hearts. Some of these obstacles we might be able to surmount, with perseverance, sacrifice and the grace of God; others we will battle with over perhaps the entire course of our lives, always falling just short of what we could achieve if only we were willing to 'let go and let God'.

But buried within the gospel passage are six precious words, which give hope to all those who struggle: 'Jesus, looking at him, loved him.' Jesus has engaged with the young man and has learnt from him all about his efforts and his priorities. He sees deep into his heart, knows all his flaws – knows too that the young man has encountered a huge obstacle – but still he loves him. He speaks with love and, no doubt, with sadness, as he is all too aware of what will be the young man's reaction to the instructions to give all he has to the poor. But still he loves him.

And still Jesus loves us. He looks into our hearts and sees our failings and our flaws, our efforts and our disasters, and he loves us. It is through that love and with that love that we will conquer and inherit the kingdom.

Questions

- What is your relationship with money and possessions? What does your bank statement say about your priorities in life?

- Are you proud or ashamed? Are these the things that challenge you or are there others, such as relationships or power? Try to think honestly about all these things.

Prayer

Lord Jesus Christ, thank you for loving us. Help us to clear away the obstacles from our paths, and give us grace to overcome those which seem to us insuperable. Amen

Wednesday 6 April

Reflecting

Romans 8:31–39

What then are we to say about these things? If God is for us, who is against us? He who did not withhold his own Son, but gave him up for all of us, will he not with him also give us everything else? Who will bring any charge against God's elect? It is God who justifies. Who is to condemn? It is Christ Jesus, who died, yes, who was raised, who is at the right hand of God, who indeed intercedes for us. Who will separate us from the love of Christ? Will hardship, or distress, or persecution, or famine, or nakedness, or peril, or sword? As it is written,

> 'For your sake we are being killed all day long;
> we are accounted as sheep to be slaughtered.'

No, in all these things we are more than conquerors through him who loved us. For I am convinced that neither death, nor life, nor angels, nor rulers, nor things present, nor things to come, nor powers, nor height, nor depth, nor anything else in all creation, will be able to separate us from the love of God in Christ Jesus our Lord.

 Reflection

We looked yesterday at the obstacles we put in the way of our relationship with God – all those things, whether material or spiritual, that we cling on to, cluttering our lives to such an extent that we are weighed down and unable to continue the journey towards the kingdom. We looked at the tragedy of the rich young man, who knew what he had to do, but found himself unable to do it, and we questioned whether we too were in that position. But just as we were about to despair, there shone out from the passage the love that Jesus had for the man, despite his failure and his flaws.

The passage today shares some of the obstacles that are put in our way not through any fault or action of our own, but simply through the working of the world: 'Hardship, or distress, or persecution, or famine, or nakedness, or peril, or sword.' Some of these are due to the action of a constantly changing creation, mending and breaking, growing and dying; some are due to the malice of our fellow human beings, and for many of them there is no action that can be taken to avoid or alleviate their effects. So how do we navigate the difficulties and sadness of our human existence? How do we hold on to hope? By raising our eyes to the God who created us, who loved us so much that he 'did not withhold his own Son, but gave him up for all of us'.

I prayed about this passage this morning, and into my mind came a picture of the wise men, travelling to witness the arrival of the Messiah, the promised one. They had no map, no certainty, no fixed destination – all they had was a star to follow. And follow it they did. T.S. Eliot's poem 'The Journey of the Magi' tells the story from the point of view of these travellers, and the hardships they encountered on the journey. He describes surly camels and mutinous camel-drivers; he helps us to picture towns and villages unused to strangers and wary of their ways; he imagines the prejudice and hostility the magi must have faced. But all the time, they kept their goal in sight, allowing nothing to distract them, confident in their destination. Homesick and regretful at times during the journey, they continue onwards and finally arrive at the birthplace of the Messiah, an arrival which with masterly understatement Eliot describes as ‘satisfactory’.

The love of God for each one of us shines like a star in the darkness. We must follow where it leads, regardless of the dangers and difficulties we encounter on the journey. God is with us as we travel – the sacrifice of Christ has ensured a complete involvement of God in and for the world. It may seem at times as if we are far from the love of God – all of us have experienced feelings of doubt, alienation, isolation and suffering, which have led us perhaps to doubt the very existence of God. It is easy to become overwhelmed by the pain of our current situation to the extent that we cannot see beyond the immediacy of our anguish. But it is at those very times that we need to lift our heads and look beyond the darkness of the present to the waves of love and light washing over us, bathing us in compassion and healing, encouraging and supporting us, sharing in the struggle, but also triumphing over it.

‘We are more than conquerors’ – the darkness of evil has been completely vanquished in our name, on our behalf. Nothing in creation can stand against God, and if he is on our side, we will be undefeated. What wonderful words of hope and reassurance – truly, if God is for us, nothing can be against us. Just as we are exhorted in the words of Deuteronomy to love God, so we can remind ourselves daily of God’s great love for us: nothing ‘in all creation will be able to separate us from the love of God in Christ Jesus our Lord.’

Questions

- Think of the times when you have felt separated from God – what were the occasions? How did you overcome your feelings of doubt and despair?
- What gives you hope in your times of darkness?

Prayer

Lord, help me to hold fast to your love. Let nothing that the world can throw at me obscure your light. Give me faith to believe and courage to move forward, even when all seems dark, to seek your love. Amen

Thursday 7 April

Living

Ruth 4:13–17

So Boaz took Ruth and she became his wife. When they came together, the Lord made her conceive, and she bore a son. Then the women said to Naomi, 'Blessed be the Lord, who has not left you this day without next-of-kin; and may his name be renowned in Israel! He shall be to you a restorer of life and a nourisher of your old age; for your daughter-in-law who loves you, who is more to you than seven sons, has borne him.' Then Naomi took the child and laid him in her bosom, and became his nurse. The women of the neighbourhood gave him a name, saying, 'A son has been born to Naomi.' They named him Obed; he became the father of Jesse, the father of David.

Reflection

The book of Ruth has been described as the only book in the Bible where every character behaves themselves. It is a beautiful, heart-warming story which gives those who read it today an opportunity to understand better what it was like to live in Old Testament times. It is the story of two women, Ruth and Naomi, who leave one homeland to return to the homeland of the other; the shelter they find there due to the generosity of a relative, Boaz; and the new life they build there, which blends with the family tree of Jesse to form part of the genealogy of Christ. All the action takes place in rural settings, with the rhythm of seed time and harvest, hard labour and celebration, a backdrop to the main events. These events are strikingly similar to those with which we engage today – the struggle to earn a living (even though we might not have to grow our own food); the challenge of living relationships, balancing family loyalties against personal need; looking to the future in order to protect the present.

But the joy of the book is that it possesses an extra dimension, in that the prayer life of each character and their relationship with God suffuses the entire narrative. Each action is set within a wholehearted, grounded faith. Each response takes into account the obligation of all created beings to their creator. Naomi sends Orpah back to Moab with prayer: 'The Lord grant that you may find security, each of you in the house of your husband' (1:9). Boaz greets his workers with prayer: 'The Lord be with you!' And they call back, 'The Lord bless you' (2:4). Boaz's welcome to Ruth includes prayer: 'May the Lord reward you for your deeds' (2:12). And Naomi greets Ruth's news of Boaz with prayer: 'Blessed be he by the Lord' (2:20). Boaz responds to Ruth's brave visit with prayer: 'May you be blessed by the Lord, my daughter' (3:10). A prayer is said on the occasion of their marriage: 'May the Lord make the woman who is coming into your house like Rachel and Leah, who together built up the house of Israel' (4:11–12). And finally, Ruth's baby son is given to Naomi with prayer: 'Blessed be the Lord!' (4:14).

Because of the depth of their relationship with God, each character is able to take the traditions of the Old Testament laws and, infusing them with loving sacrifice, transform them into life-giving situations and relationships. When the widowed Moabite Ruth follows her mother-in-law Naomi back to her homeland, she takes the tradition of kinship and loyalty to its logical conclusion. Concerned that an elderly woman is making the journey alone, she accompanies and protects her. Boaz follows the Levitical laws which require reapers to leave crops for gleaning, but goes one step further by giving instructions for the reapers to leave all fallen grain. As part of their covenant with God, the children of Israel must show the same charity to others that he showed to them, but in the book of Ruth, legal obligation becomes the loving recognition of common humanity.

What Naomi and Ruth need is someone to protect their future, to ensure that they no longer have to rely on the scraps of others' generosity but can grow and flourish in a safe future. Boaz takes on this role of protector, giving Ruth and Naomi a home and security and in due course a son to carry on the name. Thus three generous, self-sacrificing individuals, prepared to go the extra mile in the service of others, find a place in the history of the Messiah.

Our place, too, is waiting for us – all that we need do is put ourselves trustingly under the protection of God. In response to his loving sacrifice for us, we will open our hearts and our lives to others, responding generously and willingly to their needs, giving not only what is required of us, but more besides, in recognition of all that was first given to us. Nor should we forget that Ruth, a Moabite, first gets to know God through knowing Naomi: 'Your people shall be my people, and your God my God' (1:16). We do not know whose lives we will influence by our actions, nor who will learn of God's ways through our behaviour, so everything we say or do must echo God's loving intentions for all humanity.

Questions

- When did you last go the extra mile for someone? How can you do that today?
- Who do you know who has gone the extra mile for you? Thank God for them.

Prayer

Loving Lord, help me to live so that my actions are a witness to your love. Help me to give all that is asked of me, and more, since it is only through your generosity that I can truly live. Amen

Friday 8 April

Telling

Deuteronomy 6:1–9

Now this is the commandment – the statutes and the ordinances – that the Lord your God charged me to teach you to observe in the land that you are about to cross into and occupy, so that you and your children and your children's children may fear the Lord your God all the days of your life, and keep all his decrees and his commandments that I am commanding you, so that your days may be long. Hear therefore, O Israel, and observe them diligently, so that it may go well with you, and so that you may multiply greatly in a land flowing with milk and honey, as the Lord, the God of your ancestors, has promised you.

Hear, O Israel: The Lord is our God, the Lord alone. You shall love the Lord your God with all your heart, and with all your soul, and with all your might. Keep these words that I am commanding you today in your heart. Recite them to your children and talk about them when you are at home and when you are away, when you lie down and when you rise. Bind them as a sign on your hand, fix them as an emblem on your forehead, and write them on the doorposts of your house and on your gates.

Reflection

One of the joys of being a parish priest is the accompanying involvement in schools. Many of the parishes in which I served had primary schools in the local community and most of these had some relationship with the Church of England. This relationship has a long history, since education has remained closely tied to religion for many hundreds of years. Monasteries were centres of literacy, a skill that was promulgated as religious institutions founded schools and universities – Winchester College in 1382, Eton College in 1440, and so on. On a smaller scale, local churches also began developing systems of educating parishioners in the understanding of Christianity.

With its displacement of people from systems of feudal connection and responsibility into the largely unregulated industrial towns, the Industrial Revolution precipitated the breakdown of these informal arrangements, leading to large sectors of people who were illiterate. This was first addressed in a systematic way by Robert Raikes in 1781, who was disturbed by the large groups of children apparently running wild in his local town. On being told it was worse on Sundays, when the factories were closed, Raikes began a programme of education on Sundays, from 10.00 am to 12.00 pm and then from 1.00 pm to 5.30 pm, 'and then to be dismissed, with an injunction to go home quietly, and by no means to make a noise in the street'.

Nowadays many local schools are still affiliated to the church, and work in partnership with the parish priest to share something of gospel values with the pupils and their families. For me, this mostly took the form of leading regular assemblies, and I relished the weekly visit to the village primary school to tell the Bible stories that I knew so well to the next generation of listeners.

Primary school children are an excellent training ground for storytellers. If a story captures the pupils' imagination, there is a breathless attention in the room as every detail is seized upon. If, however, the story lacks pace or fails to ignite a spark of interest, a group of children will soon disintegrate into a wriggling, fidgeting mass, as they look to whispered conversations with friends or the contents of their pockets for means of passing the time until the assembly is over. I quickly learnt that the addition of small, interesting details will hold their attention, as well as accompanying actions to highlight salient points in the narrative. I acquired the skill of drawing a story to a rapid close if I could see that it had gone on long enough, and I also learnt to begin and end with the learning point, as well as reinforcing it somewhere in the middle of the narrative, in order to be sure it would reach as many ears as possible.

The stories would often be grouped around Christian values, such as respect, patience and trust, and these in turn all rested on the two commandments which Jesus gave us – to love God and to love our neighbour. Every story, every anecdote, every learning point was built upon these two foundation stones of our faith, as I tried to share how people might express them in their everyday lives.

Not all of us will be fortunate enough to work with young children, helping them to discover the principles and values upon which a Christian life is based. But many of us will have some contact with children, whether through families, neighbours or church communities. We can all help to reinforce the key elements of faith in Christ.

Some of us can buy our young relations Bible story books. There is a wonderful range and scope available, so there is bound to be something to capture the imagination of a small child. As the child grows, we can help them access the sort of books which explore faith and its implications for teenagers or young adults.

We can be on hand to answer their questions, treating their enquiries with respect and consideration.

We can offer to help with children's and youth programmes at church, which are often sadly lacking in volunteers. Sometimes this lack is simply due to an insufficient number of people willing to spend time with youngsters, often from the mistaken belief that in order to reach young people one must be of a similar age. If we cast our minds back to our own childhood and youth we will doubtless soon realise that many of the most influential people in our lives were not young at all, but had the wisdom of age and the experience of a long life well lived.

Above all, however, it is our words and deeds that will tell the best story – the most accurate and relevant. If we do truly 'keep them in our hearts', they will emerge in speech and action and reach the hearts of others as well.

Questions

- How do you live out loving God and neighbour 'with all your heart, with all your soul and with all your might'?
- How might you help others to learn what that means?
- How might you enable the next generation to access the Bible and all its riches?

Prayer

> *Stronger by weakness, wiser men become*
> *as they draw nearer to their eternal home.*
> Samuel Johnson (1709–84)

God of young and old alike, help me to share my faith. Give me courage to speak out, a willingness to help others and the opportunities to share with others all that my belief has meant to me. Amen

Saturday 9 April

Sharing

John 11:1–6, 30–37

Now a certain man was ill, Lazarus of Bethany, the village of Mary and her sister Martha. Mary was the one who anointed the Lord with perfume and wiped his feet with her hair; her brother Lazarus was ill. So the sisters sent a message to Jesus, 'Lord, he whom you love is ill.' But when Jesus heard it, he said, 'This illness does not lead to death; rather it is for God's glory, so that the Son of God may be glorified through it.' Accordingly, though Jesus loved Martha and her sister and Lazarus, after having heard that Lazarus was ill, he stayed two days longer in the place where he was...

Now Jesus had not yet come to the village, but was still at the place where Martha had met him. The Jews who were with her in the house, consoling her, saw Mary get up quickly and go out. They followed her because they thought that she was going to the tomb to weep there. When Mary came where Jesus was and saw him, she knelt at his feet and said to him, 'Lord, if you had been here, my brother would not have died.' When Jesus saw her weeping, and the Jews who came with her also weeping, he was greatly disturbed in spirit and deeply moved. He said, 'Where have you laid him?' They said to him, 'Lord, come and see.' Jesus began to weep. So the Jews said, 'See how he loved him!' But some of them said, 'Could not he who opened the eyes of the blind man have kept this man from dying?'

Reflection

Rembrandt's famous painting *The Raising of Lazarus* is powerful and awe inspiring, full of dark, rich colour, with the faces of the main characters illuminated by some far-off light source. Jesus is pictured standing before the open grave, his right arm raised in a pose of power and confidence. His mouth is open as if he is speaking those commanding words with which he summoned Lazarus from his tomb: 'Lazarus, come out!' (John 11:43). Mary and Martha are on Jesus' right, placed lower than him in the picture. Their mouths too are open, but with awe and wonder. And at the bottom of the picture, half risen from the grave is the ghastly white figure of Lazarus, still haggard from his last illness, wrapped in white cloths which contrast sharply with the dark line of the tombstone. His gaze is fixed on Jesus as if it is only through his strength that Lazarus can move out of the deep trench in which he is placed. Viewers of the painting are left in no doubt as to the significance of what is happening here, nor the impact of the event upon all who witnessed it.

In contrast to this is Vincent van Gogh's *The Raising of Lazarus (after Rembrandt)*. While being treated for mental illness in an asylum, van Gogh had been sent a print of Rembrandt's painting by his brother Theodore. Clearly it had sparked his imagination, but the resulting picture seems to me, and I am by no means an art critic, to bear very little resemblance to that of Rembrandt's dark, brooding images. The palette of van Gogh is bright yellows and greens, with streaks of fiery orange; the brush strokes are short and vigorous, clearly defined in that unique style of his. The picture throbs with light and energy, as the two women, arms raised in astonishment, lean close to Lazarus as if to help him from his resting place. Lazarus looks dazed and half awake, but he is already beginning to move out of the tomb, ready to take on life once more. There is no sign of Jesus, but the sun (the Son) has a central place in the picture, its vivid yellow and orange light sending swirling rays of pattern and colour radiating over the scene.

The same subject, two very different interpretations – but perhaps one message. Jesus has been brought to the tomb of Lazarus by his distraught sisters, torn apart by their grief. They are hoping wildly that Jesus can help them, can change the dreadful fate which has overwhelmed them. They have appealed to his friendship and his love for the family, and he in return has been greatly moved by the depths of their sorrow. But now the focus is on Lazarus and the charge is given him to leave the tomb, to remove his grave wrappings and to take up once more the mantle of life and love. And Lazarus responds. He responds with awe, with confusion, with willingness, with a gaze fixed on Christ and with an awareness of his sisters witnessing the incredible event. Lazarus leaves the grave and lives once more.

This scene leaves us in no doubt that Jesus lived among us, sharing our grief and sorrows as he shared our joy and celebration. It is from moments like this that we can put our faith in the one who journeys alongside us, experiencing all that we do, while holding us in his tender, protective love. There can be no doubt as to his power either – the Son of God can call forth souls who have already begun their journey after death. This was no act of resuscitation, as Lazarus had been dead for three days. This was a bringing back from the dead – a resurrection. And what does it take for this to happen? A heartfelt plea – 'Lord, he whom you love is ill' (v. 3) – and a declaration of faith – 'Yes, Lord, I believe that you are the Messiah, the Son of God, the one coming into the world' (v. 27). Then comes the summons to new life, with renewed hope and energy, brimming with love.

This story is given to us that we might understand just what is being offered to us by Christ, as he invites us to share in his life through the Holy Spirit, who dwells within all of us. Are we brave enough to step out of the darkness and half-life of the tomb, to strip off the grave clothes of worldly preoccupations which entangle us and step gladly into the Son-lit world which is ours should we choose to accept it?

Questions

- Find images of the paintings by Rembrandt and van Gogh. Spend some time simply looking at and reflecting on them, noticing the details as well as the impact of the whole. Which one calls to you most?

- What tangles around you like the wrappings of Lazarus' grave clothes? How might you free yourself?

Prayer

Lord, lead me to the new life which is mine. Help me to say in response to your calling that I believe that you are the Son of God, the Messiah. Amen

Sunday 10 April (Palm Sunday)

Becoming

John 12:20–26

Now among those who went up to worship at the festival were some Greeks. They came to Philip, who was from Bethsaida in Galilee, and said to him, 'Sir, we wish to see Jesus.' Philip went and told Andrew; then Andrew and Philip went and told Jesus. Jesus answered them, 'The hour has come for the Son of Man to be glorified. Very truly, I tell you, unless a grain of wheat falls into the earth and dies, it remains just a single grain; but if it dies, it bears much fruit. Those who love their life lose it, and those who hate their life in this world will keep it for eternal life. Whoever serves me must follow me, and where I am, there will my servant be also. Whoever serves me, the Father will honour.'

Reflection

The February 2021 issue of the *European Journal of Social Psychology* includes an article entitled 'An exploration of spiritual superiority: the paradox of self-enhancement'. In the article, Professor Roos Vonk reports on her research into the effect of mindfulness and other spiritual practices on the practitioner. She discovered that, although the aim of such practices was to reduce the ego and to make people more aware of their place within the wider universe, in fact the opposite was true. A sense of 'spiritual superiority' was endemic among those who meditated, as well as a feeling of self-satisfaction at their heightened spiritual awareness and sensitivity. Over 3,500 people were given a questionnaire and the results demonstrated that the human ego is a truly powerful thing – the very practices designed to reduce it led people to feel that they had achieved something others had not and thus enhanced their self-esteem and feeling of self-worth.

Christians are no less susceptible to such feelings of spiritual superiority. There are huge dangers inherent in gathering together in self-selecting groups, singing hymns and choruses in the style that we prefer and listening to sermons and lectures which support our sense of having access to the more important issues in life. These habits reinforce our notion that our way is the one true way, whether that be when and how we worship, what charities we support or simply how we react to the challenges and issues of the everyday world.

How easy it is to shut out those who disagree, who follow a different path, who are unable to fit in with what we are doing or who feel uncomfortable with our social or spiritual practices. How often must we remind ourselves of Jesus' words here – a stark warning to all who embark upon an exploration of the Christian life expecting it to be easy or comfortable, bringing with it only benefits and pleasures: 'Those who love their life lose it.' Those who really seek to develop a deep and lasting relationship with God must be prepared to give up everything in its pursuit. Those who truly want to follow Christ must follow wherever he leads – even to death. Only when the self-centred, self-seeking part of ourselves has truly been put to death can the seed of eternal life germinate and begin to grow.

And what of the Greeks who asked to see Jesus? What were they expecting? Miracles, perhaps. A healing or two. Some wise words maybe wrapped up in a parable – preferably one which was challenging but not too unnerving, one which held the interest but did not demand too much else. What did they get? A man preparing for death. A man who knew that in six days he would be crucified. A man who knew that his followers, too, must sacrifice much in order to gain even more, but that there would be pain indeed in the sacrifice.

On this Palm Sunday, the beginning of Holy Week, we are reminded that Jesus chose not to enter Jerusalem in triumph, riding on a charger, but humbly on the back of a donkey, aligning himself with the outcast, those on the edge, sharing every part of our lives – the humdrum as well as the glamorous.

We cannot just 'see' Jesus. We cannot simply pick the words and practices that appeal to us, choosing to go with the feel-good habits of giving to the poor, helping the needy and maybe becoming part of a community of like-minded people in order to feel better about ourselves, superior to the common herd. Following Jesus requires going where he leads, loving God and loving our neighbour even when that is what we want to do least, even when we consider them undeserving of our love. The cost is indeed high. But the rewards are greater still.

Questions

- When have you been guilty of 'spiritual superiority'? Is it easier to spot it in others rather than yourself?
- What would you say to someone who tells you they want to see Jesus?

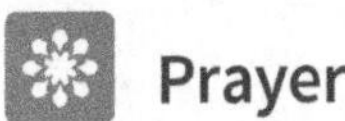

Prayer

O Jesus, thou hast promised
to all who follow thee
that where thou art in glory
there shall thy servant be.
And, Jesus, I have promised
to serve thee to the end;
O give me grace to follow,
my Master and my friend
John Bode (1816–74)

Most Almighty God, you hold in your hand the earth and all that is in it. Here is my life. It is precious to you, I know. Help me to trust that I can rest in the shadow of your wings And that you will hold me safe. Amen

Questions for group study

- Reflecting on this week's Bible passages, which ones have engaged you most? Which have you found most challenging? Has your understanding of love changed and, if so, how?

- Julian of Norwich wrote: 'Learn it well: Love was His meaning... Hold thee therein and thou shalt learn and know more in the same.' How can we hold ourselves in love?

- What obstacles lie in the path of your journey with God?

Creative prayer

You will need a piece of paper and a pencil or crayons.

Make an 'altar cloth'. Divide the paper into squares of roughly equal size. Into each of those squares write or draw something that you wish to bring before God – the faces of those you love, perhaps, or those you do not; those you have hurt or those you have been hurt by. When you have drawn all you want to, hold your 'altar cloth' and ask God for the grace to place your life into his hands.

Holy Week | Monday 11 April–Sunday 17 April

Changing

We are now in Holy Week, that most solemn and beautiful of weeks in the church calendar. My readings are not perhaps traditional for Holy Week, but ones which will reflect how far we have journeyed in the process of learning to understand and share our Christian story. This amazing series of events is the culmination of one journey – the earth-bound life of Christ – and the beginning of another – a new, exciting journey into the heart of love and the eternal kingdom.

Monday 11 April

Listening

Isaiah 42:1–9

Here is my servant, whom I uphold,
    my chosen, in whom my soul delights;
I have put my spirit upon him;
    he will bring forth justice to the nations.
He will not cry or lift up his voice,
    or make it heard in the street;
a bruised reed he will not break,
    and a dimly burning wick he will not quench;
    he will faithfully bring forth justice.
He will not grow faint or be crushed
    until he has established justice in the earth;
    and the coastlands wait for his teaching.

Thus says God, the Lord,
    who created the heavens and stretched them out,
    who spread out the earth and what comes from it,
who gives breath to the people upon it
    and spirit to those who walk in it:
I am the Lord, I have called you in righteousness,
    I have taken you by the hand and kept you;
I have given you as a covenant to the people,
    a light to the nations,
    to open the eyes that are blind,
to bring out the prisoners from the dungeon,
    from the prison those who sit in darkness.

I am the Lord, that is my name;
my glory I give to no other,
nor my praise to idols.
See, the former things have come to pass,
and new things I now declare;
before they spring forth,
I tell you of them.

Reflection

What a beautiful song this is! I imagine it sung out loud, echoing across all lands and nations, bringing love and hope to all who are worn out by the suffering of this world. Perhaps this song means all the more to me because I am feeling weary myself as I write this; there are times in the lives of all ministers when leading a church takes a toll both physical and mental, and the body and soul are in need of rest. In such times, I turn to the Psalms and the prophecies of Isaiah that bring hope and the promise of easier times.

The writer of this song certainly knew all about soul-crushing weariness. It is believed that the song was written during a time of great turmoil and unhappiness for the children of Israel. The temple in Jerusalem had been destroyed, and many of the inhabitants of Judah had been forced into exile in Babylon. They were leaderless, adrift in a time of confusion, with no clear plan for the future. And so the prophet brought hope in the form of the servant who delights the very soul of God.

Christians often equate this servant with Christ, but the servant can equally be a general term for all the people of Israel, any community which comes together to worship God and serve him by serving his children. We are promised a leader who will act gently and with compassion: the weak and the helpless won't be battered or bullied by him; he won't threaten those who disagree with him but will instead walk gently alongside them, refusing to be threatened or bullied himself as he commits himself to working tirelessly for justice in the earth. We will be comforted by this servant. We will be nurtured and sustained. We will be freed from the fortresses of our own making, in which we have enclosed ourselves in darkness – surrounding ourselves with the prison bars of obsession with power, status, material objects and worldly success.

And we in our turn will become the servants of God, as we become aware of the life-giving breath of God being breathed upon us so gently, filling us with the Holy Spirit, enabling us to join in the work of peace and justice which began in Christ and continues in his children, inspired by his Spirit. We too will be taken by the hand and led gently in the ways of righteousness. We too will be given the grace to become a light to our communities, however small, however insignificant in the eyes of the world.

Today is the Monday of Holy Week – the beginning of the countdown to the crucifixion and resurrection, pivotal moments in the history of creation. We draw a deep breath, preparing to journey in our imagination into the final days on earth of our Lord and Saviour. We will need strong hearts and determined wills, because the events that will unfold will be heart-rending and terrible. But we will find our strength in these words, written down for us so many centuries ago to reassure and hearten, to encourage and give hope. We will not let our footsteps falter because our journey companion will walk alongside us as we travel into the heart of darkness and beyond, following the servant of all, rejoicing in his saving work.

Questions

- What does justice mean to you? Is Christian justice different to that of the world? How might you help to establish justice within your own community or household?
- From where do you gain strength and comfort when you are worn out and weary? How might you comfort others in a similar situation?

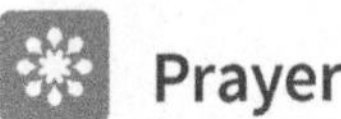

Prayer

When peace like a river attendeth my way,
when sorrows like sea billows roll;
whatever my lot, thou hast taught me to say,
'It is well, it is well with my soul.'
Horatio Spafford (1828–88)

Heavenly Father, give me your peace so that I may navigate the rivers of this earthly life with confidence in your loving purposes for me. Help me to feel the touch of your hand as you lead me, and open my eyes to your light. Amen

Tuesday 12 April

Understanding

Ecclesiastes 3:1–13

For everything there is a season, and a time for every matter under heaven:

a time to be born, and a time to die;
a time to plant, and a time to pluck up what is planted;
a time to kill, and a time to heal;
a time to break down, and a time to build up;
a time to weep, and a time to laugh;
a time to mourn, and a time to dance;
a time to throw away stones, and a time to gather stones
together;
a time to embrace, and a time to refrain from embracing;
a time to seek, and a time to lose;
a time to keep, and a time to throw away;
a time to tear, and a time to sew;
a time to keep silence, and a time to speak;
a time to love, and a time to hate;
a time for war, and a time for peace.

What gain have the workers from their toil? I have seen the business that God has given to everyone to be busy with. He has made everything suitable for its time; moreover he has put a sense of past and future into their minds, yet they cannot find out what God has done from the beginning to the end. I know that there is nothing better for them than to be happy and enjoy themselves as long as they live; moreover, it is God's gift that all should eat and drink and take pleasure in all their toil.

Reflection

On 15 April 2019 a fire broke out in the roof of the Cathedral of Notre Dame in Paris. Like many others, I watched with horror the events of that Monday evening as one of the most important buildings in France caught fire, huge orange flames gradually devouring the Parisian landmark, which had been part of the city skyline for over 850 years. The following morning, I read with relief the news that a lot of the structure remained and that the building would continue to be the point from where all distances in France were measured, the heart of France. I saw the pictures – the skeleton of the roof in flames, the weeping crowd who witnessed it.

Why does the fate of this building strike a chord in the hearts of not just French citizens but people across the world? Because it is a symbol of survival, perhaps, something which has witnessed revolution, invasion and terrorism and yet remained intact. Because it is a symbol of something greater than the daily compulsion to find food and warmth and to procreate so that the genes can continue. Because it points to something more than the individual, something greater than ourselves, uniting us to look beyond our own existence. And because it is a sign of the inextinguishable nature of the Christian faith, which has survived across the centuries, battered, attacked and finally left to crumble almost to nothing beneath the weight of the cynicism and selfishness which is the prevailing mood of so many people's lives today.

Not just today, perhaps. Even though Jesus predicted his death – and resurrection – several times across his ministry, the news that God had raised Jesus from the grave and defeated death and the devil was utterly shocking. No one expects resurrection, and no one believes it at first. And who can blame them? Resurrection doesn't simply mean that Jesus was brought back to life, as he did with Lazarus. The resurrection of Christ claims that God entered human history not only to redeem it but also to create an entirely new reality.

This is frightening. Of all the rules we can expect, including those of the litany of Ecclesiastes, we do at least expect the dead to stay dead. The rules may be harsh, but they are predictable, safe and reassuring. Resurrection overturns it all. The fact of the resurrection affects all our reality, not just our faith. As C.S. Lewis writes, 'I believe in Christianity as I believe that the sun has risen: not only because I see it, but because by it I see everything else.'

Death does not have the final word. Love and life are stronger than fear and death. We can expect to see those we've loved and lost again. God has a future in store for each and all of us. Anything is possible with God.

The image of the gold cross shining through the darkness of the nave of Notre Dame is stronger than that of the spire tumbling into the orange flames. New hope is being held out to the people of France, a restoration programme is underway. Perhaps now others will not take for granted those symbols of hope in their own landscapes and what they stand for – the promises of a better future, the assurance of companionship on our often-lonely journey through this world.

Perhaps now the world will look to its own buildings of faith and care for them better, aware that their loss would mean so much more than the absence of bricks and mortar. Perhaps now we will take our own faith more seriously, as something that changes not just our lives but also the lives of whole communities for the better. These changes are often undervalued and ignored. The effect of people who believe in a God who loves and values every human being is not always discernible until it disappears. We must ensure, through our own words and actions, that it never does.

Questions

- What does your church building mean to you?
- Do you think you really appreciate the enormity of the resurrection? Do you see everything else through its lens?

Prayer

Lord God, as I journey through life, help me to view all events and activities, all emotions and actions, through the fact of your resurrection. Amen

Wednesday 13 April

Reflecting

John 13:2–7, 12–17

During supper Jesus, knowing that the Father had given all things into his hands, and that he had come from God and was going to God, got up from the table, took off his outer robe, and tied a towel around himself. Then he poured water into a basin and began to wash the disciples' feet and to wipe them with the towel that was tied around him. He came to Simon Peter, who said to him, 'Lord, are you going to wash my feet?' Jesus answered, 'You do not know now what I am doing, but later you will understand'...

After he had washed their feet, had put on his robe, and had returned to the table, he said to them, 'Do you know what I have done to you? You call me Teacher and Lord – and you are right, for that is what I am. So if I, your Lord and Teacher, have washed your feet, you also ought to wash one another's feet. For I have set you an example, that you also should do as I have done to you. Very truly, I tell you, servants are not greater than their master, nor are messengers greater than the one who sent them. If you know these things, you are blessed if you do them.'

Reflection

Some years ago, I visited a large church, grand and imposing, which prided itself on carrying out all rites and rituals in the most exquisite fashion, with as much pomp and circumstance as could be mustered. I was present for the service on Maundy Thursday, and witnessed the most elaborate foot-washing ceremony I have ever seen. The celebrant carefully removed his magnificent gold-embroidered chasuble and laid it on a large wooden bench set there for the purpose. Then, clothed in his white cassock-alb, he carefully knotted a white linen apron around his waist. Next to him stood a server who had a white linen cloth draped over one arm and reverently held a vast china basin. The celebrant then proceeded towards a group of four people who were waiting ready with one clean bare foot held out. This foot was taken, wiped with a white cloth then dried briefly with the towel before the celebrant moved to the next foot.

Although I deeply appreciated the symbolism of the ritual, and thoroughly acknowledged its power as a gesture of servanthood on the part of the celebrant, I could not help wondering at how far we had travelled since that first foot washing. Gathered in an upper room, supper laid out ready, the weary, dusty travellers must have sighed with relief as they unlatched their sandals to let their sore feet rest. What alarm they must have felt as each in turn had those travel-stained feet grasped lovingly by their Master and tenderly bathed so that they were clean and refreshed for their meal. What a lesson in leadership did Jesus give them as he demonstrated in the most practical of ways what it meant to serve others.

For me, the modern-day equivalent is not the ceremony of foot-washing in a grand church, although that may well be helpful to many. Rather, it's the sight that greets me when I visit a home for the elderly and those with dementia. I see a group of human beings who can no longer care for themselves being cared for by others, helped to do those things they used to do but are unable to now. It's when

I observe husbands and wives gently coaxing reluctant eaters, spooning nourishment into their mouths with words of encouragement and love. It's when I see husbands and wives, sons and daughters, holding hands and murmuring anecdotes about their day, not hopeful of a response because for many the time for response has passed, but offering love just the same, without obvious return.

By washing the feet of his disciples, Jesus modelled an attitude of loving service which we are all enjoined to copy: 'If I, your Lord and Teacher, have washed your feet, you also ought to wash one another's feet.' Some of us may have to do this literally – we may have young children, elderly relatives or sick or disabled friends who cannot perform such tasks by themselves and must be ministered to. But the principle extends much further than simply helping with practical tasks. A servant to others reaches out to those in need despite the cost to themselves. A servant to others listens closely and tries to help with what is wanted, rather than assuming they know what is wanted and offering it regardless. A servant to others puts those others before themselves, not being falsely humble or hoping for recognition but in genuine response to the one who first showed us how to serve.

Like Simon Peter, we may not fully understand all that we are asked to do, but like Peter we must listen to the promptings of our hearts and follow them. Then we will be blessed in the midst of being a blessing to others.

Questions

- In what ways do you practise servanthood? Are there ways in which you could do more?
- Who has been a servant to you? Thank God for them – and maybe thank them too.

Prayer

Put on then, as God's chosen ones, holy and beloved, compassion, kindness, lowliness, meekness and patience.
COLOSSIANS 3:12 (RSV)

Heavenly Father, give me the gift of servanthood, that I may serve others and in so doing, serve you. Amen

Thursday 14 April (Maundy Thursday)

Living

John 13:31–35

When he had gone out, Jesus said, 'Now the Son of Man has been glorified, and God has been glorified in him. If God has been glorified in him, God will also glorify him in himself and will glorify him at once. Little children, I am with you only a little longer. You will look for me; and as I said to the Jews so now I say to you, "Where I am going, you cannot come." I give you a new commandment, that you love one another. Just as I have loved you, you also should love one another. By this everyone will know that you are my disciples, if you have love for one another.'

Reflection

I have spent some time recently pondering the phenomenon of the selfie – a photo of oneself that is usually posted on social media. In one respect they are rather nauseating. What is it about people nowadays that makes it all about them? Have we really become so self-obsessed that no picture is worthy of comment unless it contains our own image? What happened to the virtue of self-effacement, of modesty? On the other hand, the selfie is very useful. When my in-laws died, my husband brought back hundreds of photographs from their house, thousands perhaps, consisting of monument after monument, view after view of the places they had visited on trips and holidays. There was no indication of where they were or when they were taken. How much more interesting would the photos have been if either Bill or Jean, or both of them, had been in them. We would have seen them newly together, growing up, having Jeremy, growing old. Instead all we have are outdated scenes.

A selfie, therefore, establishes the importance of the individual. It is a statement – here I am; don't ignore me; I am an individual. And this is an important, even vital, statement, which reaches right to the heart of our fears and anxieties. Amid a globalised economy, in a world which deals in vast numbers, a selfie is a small voice shouting out in the media wilderness – here is a person who matters. That is a deep truth, because when we stop noticing people and stop believing individuals matter, atrocities occur and the way is open to genocide and crimes against humanity.

This is one of the reasons I am proud to be a Christian – it is a faith which asserts strongly that every individual matters. Augustine once observed that God loves each of us as if there were only one of us. In other words, Jesus radically individualised the affection he acted out towards others, never failing to focus on the particular and the unique in each human being. This represents an extraordinary commitment and discipline, especially because, even in Jesus' day, he came in contact with many, many people and so must have found it tempting to lump people together into categories and be blind to the genuine uniqueness of each human being.

I love the story of the woman with the haemorrhage, who reached out to Christ for healing. Even though he was on his way somewhere else and was surrounded by a huge crowd of people, who all had needs, Jesus stopped, took time, approached the woman with love and healed her:

> Immediately aware that power had gone forth from him, Jesus turned about in the crowd and said, 'Who touched my clothes?' And his disciples said to him, 'You see the crowd pressing in on you; how can you say, "Who touched me?"'
>
> MARK 5:30

But Jesus did. He came to the aid of the poor and the lame, the outcast and the forgotten, and he loved them all for the unique individuals that they were.

'Love one another as I have loved you.' Jesus says these words just after Judas has left the Passover table to betray Jesus. Time after time, Jesus has given Judas the chance to change his mind. As Jesus sat down with his disciples, he told them that one of them would betray him. And when the beloved disciple asked who it was, Jesus was able to give him a sign. Jesus dipped a morsel of bread in the wine and gave it to Judas. This not only indicated the betrayer, but it also offered him a final chance to repent. But more than this, it was a gesture of love. Despite the betrayal, despite the hatred, bitterness, envy or disappointment – whatever it was that motivated Judas – Jesus cut through it all with his offering of love.

Such great love is impossible to replicate. But we are made in the image of God, and loving each other as if there were none other in all the world is at least an ideal to which we can aspire, even if it remains out of our reach this side of eternity.

Question

- Who are you going to love today?

Prayer

My song is love unknown,
my Saviour's love to me;
love to the loveless shown,
that they might lovely be.
O who am I,
that for my sake
my Lord should take
frail flesh and die?

Samuel Crossman (1623–83)

Thank you, Lord, for loving me. Help me to love others in the same way. Amen

Friday 15 April (Good Friday)

Telling

Mark 15:42–43; 16:1–8

When evening had come, and since it was the day of Preparation, that is, the day before the sabbath, Joseph of Arimathea, a respected member of the council, who was also himself waiting expectantly for the kingdom of God, went boldly to Pilate and asked for the body of Jesus...

When the sabbath was over, Mary Magdalene, and Mary the mother of James, and Salome bought spices, so that they might go and anoint him. And very early on the first day of the week, when the sun had risen, they went to the tomb. They had been saying to one another, 'Who will roll away the stone for us from the entrance to the tomb?' When they looked up, they saw that the stone, which was very large, had already been rolled back. As they entered the tomb, they saw a young man, dressed in a white robe, sitting on the right side; and they were alarmed. But he said to them, 'Do not be alarmed; you are looking for Jesus of Nazareth, who was crucified. He has been raised; he is not here. Look, there is the place they laid him. But go, tell his disciples and Peter that he is going ahead of you to Galilee; there you will see him, just as he told you.' So they went out and fled from the tomb, for terror and amazement had seized them; and they said nothing to anyone, for they were afraid.

Reflection

You may have noticed that I have not used the traditional readings for Good Friday. I have not used the ones which speak about the crucifixion, as the events of Good Friday do not end with Jesus' death, but with his burial. In Mark's gospel, the burial is quickly followed by the resurrection, told in his usual brief style. Today's passage comes right at the end of Mark's gospel. Well, nearly at the end – in our Bibles it continues for another eight verses. But research that has been done on the text has concluded that the gospel as written by Mark actually ends here, in a strange and almost fumbling fashion. The final phrase in Greek is '*ephobounto gar*' – 'for they were afraid'.

What sort of an ending is this? Think back to the endings of other stories you know. Usually they are profoundly satisfactory – loose ends are tied up, sometimes there is a romantic fade-out or some moralising and you are left well aware that the end of the book has been reached. But not here. The resurrection has just taken place. The salvation of the world has been set in motion, with the apostles recruited as witnesses and participants in the reshaping of the entire universe. Then we are presented with this ridiculous, abrupt ending. It does not seem right. It does not inspire confidence. It does not give us that satisfying finish we expect.

Added to this, it is grammatically wrong. In New Testament Greek, *gar* ('for') is wrongly placed. No one ended a sentence with *gar*. It is a small, transitional word that leads into something else. It is the kind of word that slows us down so that there is space for us to draw breath and look forward to whatever comes next.

It was not long before readers of this gospel began supplying their own endings. It is easy to imagine a storyteller or scribe arriving at Mark 16:8 and not believing that Mark could have intended his last word to be *gar*. 'We know the rest of the story,' they might have thought, and added it on themselves, including the events of the risen Jesus appearing to the disciples. We can hardly see the join, so well-crafted are the last few verses. But (and this is a big but) the whole emphasis of the book is changed.

In a conventional story, the narrative is brought to a close as the characters live 'happily ever after'. Readers can safely leave the world and time of the book and return to their own world and time. Mark's gospel, ending as it does ('for they were afraid'), does not leave the reader in peace. The image of the murdered Jesus, so freshly depicted in the events of the crucifixion, is still stamped on our imaginations. Added to this is the awe-inspiring courage of Joseph of Arimathea. The day of crucifixion ends with a hasty burial, marked with pain and sorrow. And contrary to all our expectations, the day of the resurrection is no better. The women are terrified by the words of the angel, and they say nothing to anyone of what has occurred. We are still in crucifixion mode, still suffering, still afraid.

It seems to me that Mark intended *gar* as his final word. It leaves us off-balance, mid-stride. We do not know where the next step will take us – towards belief or unbelief? Will we have the courage to rearrange our whole reality in accordance with the stunning news of the resurrection, or will we run away and hide in the comfort of the everyday? Will we be drawn to worship with our hearts, minds and souls, or will we return to our earthbound selves?

There is a picture which hangs in my living room. It is a naive painting, dating probably from the 1950s, and not very well drawn. It has an angel holding a large piece of blank paper and at the bottom of the picture is a small child writing just one word, which is not visible to the viewer. At the top of the page is written: 'Your life is like a blank page. Write "yes" at the bottom and let Jesus fill in the rest.' Everything Mark has written leads us to this – an invitation to say yes or no to the risen Lord. He doesn't presume; he doesn't argue. The writer has brought a new genre of literature into being but does not wrap it up. At the last minute he steps aside, hands us the pen and says, 'Here, you write it. Write a conclusion with your life.'

The gospel story is bigger than my story, bigger than your story and bigger than the story of our church communities. And always it invites us to go on, in whatever place and in whatever circumstances we find ourselves. We must live out the resurrection truth for ourselves, with others and in love.

Questions

- Compare the ending of Mark's gospel to that of your favourite story. Which is more satisfactory? How does Mark's ending lead you onwards?

Prayer

Heavenly Father, thank you for the sacrifice of your Son. Give me the courage not to stop at the ending of death but to hope in the journey beyond. Amen

Saturday 16 April (Holy Saturday)

Sharing

Matthew 27:62–66

The next day, that is, after the day of Preparation, the chief priests and the Pharisees gathered before Pilate and said, 'Sir, we remember what that impostor said while he was still alive, "After three days I will rise again." Therefore command that the tomb be made secure until the third day; otherwise his disciples may go and steal him away, and tell the people, "He has been raised from the dead", and the last deception would be worse than the first.' Pilate said to them, 'You have a guard of soldiers; go, make it as secure as you can.' So they went with the guard and made the tomb secure by sealing the stone.

Reflection

Yesterday we thought about endings. Today, I begin with a beginning – the first line of Leo Tolstoy's *Anna Karenina*: 'Happy families are all alike; every unhappy family is unhappy in its own way.' Not a very cheerful start, but isn't it always the way that the happy Christmases, Easters and other festival days all blend into one, while the ones that are awful stand out?

And it's true – festival days can be miserable. Periods of celebration for some people almost always are times of depression for other people. Times set aside for rejoicing can become terribly troubling. My heart always goes out to those whose loved ones die just at the time of a great celebration. Forever after, Christmas or Easter, birthdays or anniversaries will be touched with more than the usual level of regret and sadness – for the loved one is not only missing but went missing at that very time, and the grief reappears, sharp and bitter.

Rereading the resurrection stories in the gospels with this reality in mind, I was surprised to find there what we experience here. The ancient biblical narratives about the resurrection of Jesus contain a mixture of ecstasy and despondency, an intermingling of delight and discouragement. Just as news of Christ's resurrection caused an explosion of joy among some believers, other believers experienced an erosion of hope. Luke tells us that on the very day of the resurrection, as word of Christ's presence swept through Jerusalem, two of his disciples were headed towards Emmaus, worn out and despondent. Even though they had heard the news of the resurrection, it meant nothing to them – they were trapped in the in-between times: 'We had hoped that he was the one to redeem Israel' (Luke 24:21), they say to the stranger who questions them.

Easter came and some people missed it. It happened in Jerusalem. It happens where we live. It happens every year. Christ rose, and not even all of his former followers realised his presence. And this is the case today. For some of us are trapped in an eternal Holy Saturday – a day when soldiers came to close the entrance to the tomb so that his grief-stricken followers could not even perform the ritual anointing of the body; a day when those who had seen and believed were shocked and crushed by the trauma of witnessing such a savage death; a day when the future which had been promised lay on the ground, shattered and broken. For some of us, the joy of Easter morning escapes us. We are caught up in grief or pain or held by memories of traumatic events. We cannot call out 'Alleluia', because there is no praise in us. We cannot grasp the truth of the resurrection, because we are held back by the lies of this world.

But this is not what the good news is about. The good news is that, whatever our emotions, however trapped we feel in a perpetual Holy Saturday, Jesus understands and loves us. The good news is that we do not have to understand Christ, because he understands us, fully and completely. We do not have to share in the rejoicing if we are unable to do so, because Christ walks alongside us in our suffering. The Prince of Peace stands with us in our conflict and chaos.

And Christ appears to us. He appears to men walking despondently to Emmaus, away from the troubles and the triumph, the disaster and the processions. He appears to grief-stricken women whose world has broken, and he will appear to us, as he always will 'where two or three are gathered in his name' (see Matthew 18:20).

The gospel is good news – but it can only be so if that news is shared. This is our task: not just to experience Christ wherever we are, however we are feeling, but also to share that experience with others. Jesus himself gives us examples – simple conversations, cheerful sharing of hospitality, easy and sympathetic companionship. Nothing drastic, nothing really difficult, just a constant, loving companionship. That's all that is needed to rescue an Easter from the bleakness of 'three-for-a-pound' chocolate eggs and transform it into the start of the joyous and challenging journey which is the Christian faith.

Questions

- Do the great festivals of the church fill you with joy or regret? How can you combine the two in your commemoration of such events? How can you reach out to others who might feel the same?

Prayer

Heavenly Father, Lord of light, hear my prayers when I cannot pray, comfort me when I am so desolate that I cannot reach out to you and uphold me when I am falling. Lord of all, hear my prayer and answer me. Amen

Sunday 17 April (Easter Sunday)

Becoming

Luke 24:1–12

But on the first day of the week, at early dawn, they came to the tomb, taking the spices that they had prepared. They found the stone rolled away from the tomb, but when they went in, they did not find the body. While they were perplexed about this, suddenly two men in dazzling clothes stood beside them. The women were terrified and bowed their faces to the ground, but the men said to them, 'Why do you look for the living among the dead? He is not here, but has risen. Remember how he told you, while he was still in Galilee, that the Son of Man must be handed over to sinners, and be crucified, and on the third day rise again.' Then they remembered his words, and returning from the tomb, they told all this to the eleven and to all the rest. Now it was Mary Magdalene, Joanna, Mary the mother of James, and the other women with them who told this to the apostles. But these words seemed to them an idle tale, and they did not believe them. But Peter got up and ran to the tomb; stooping and looking in, he saw the linen cloths by themselves; then he went home, amazed at what had happened.

Reflection

My son was not very well when he was born. During the pregnancy, a defect had been spotted during an ultrasound scan and the radiographer was alarmed. I knew the doctors were worried, because one of them reached out and touched my hand to comfort me before delivering the bad news. The syndrome which presented itself could only be verified after birth, and the final weeks of pregnancy were nerve-racking. The days after giving birth were even worse, as my tiny son was subjected to a battery of tests, some of them extremely invasive. One test, in fact, was so alarming that the doctors would not let mothers stay with their children, only the fathers (this was nearly 20 years ago). The nights were traumatic, too, as we lay awake, conjuring up scenarios each more devastating than the last.

Finally, we went to get the results of the tests. We sat in the consultant's room, and he looked at the tests, paused and cleared his throat. 'Well, Mr and Mrs Welch,' he said, 'this one's all clear. Your son is fine.' 'All clear' – two words that put an end to hopeless anxiety, soul-wrenching worry and tears wept in the darkness of the night. 'All clear'.

There are other phrases equally powerful, both good and bad – 'I'm pregnant', 'I love you', 'We've lost him.' Entire life stories built up around life-changing words. We celebrate today some of the most important words in the Christian language. The first ones are the ones said by the angel in the tomb to Mary: 'He is not here, but has risen.'

These words, too, are life-changing, and they begin their work immediately. The first ones to hear them are the women, who have crept out of their houses at dawn, anxious and afraid, tiptoeing through the streets of Jerusalem, out to the tombs where the outcasts live among the memorials to the dead. They had come to bury with him their hopes of a new way of living, their dreams of a world which was governed by justice and mercy, a kingdom of righteousness and truth. They came in fear of soldiers and reprisals, of persecution and punishment. But still they came.

To their horror, their beloved Lord and Master was not there. Instead there was an empty tomb, filled only with the cloth wrappings which they had so carefully, so lovingly, wrapped around his body. These wrappings – the things of the world, the cares and worries of earthly preoccupations, everything that binds us and blinds us to the love of God – have been thrown off, and the women are invited to do the same. Suddenly the world looks different – new, exciting and full of wonder. 'He is not here, but has risen.'

All of us who seek God, who try to live our lives as children of God, children of the promise, and who work for the kingdom are promised that we too will not perish like the grass of the field, but that we will be called into the everlasting presence of our Lord and Saviour.

People who have undergone both the experience of cancer and the joy of those words 'all clear', people who have looked death in the face and survived, say that it changes their view of life. It changes their priorities, the things they do and the goals they have. So too must the words that mark the beginning of the Christian church change our lives and redefine our priorities, if we take them at all seriously.

But it is not enough that we hear these words and they transform our lives. On hearing these words, the women remember the rest of Jesus' words. All the stories, the injunctions, the commands, everything which they had suppressed and buried in their shock and grief, it all comes back to them, for things have happened just as he promised, and now it is their turn. The women head at once to the rest of the disciples: 'Then they remembered his words, and returning from the tomb, they told all this to the eleven and to all the rest.'

We too must hear these words: 'He is not here, but has risen.' Hear them properly, take them into our hearts and live by them. And then we must share this wonderful story, because the news is too good to keep to ourselves!

Epilogue: The never-ending story

And so we arrive at Easter Sunday, the climax of our story – and yet not the end. The wonder of the empty tomb must continue to send its echoes into our daily lives, as we take up the message it sings to us and sing it in our turn, sharing the story of God's loving purposes for every one of his children. The story of our faith journey is as long as the journey of our lives, ending only when we arrive at our final destination and can enter through the gate of our heavenly home to the place which Jesus Christ has prepared for us.

My prayer for you is that the disciplines of daily study and reflection and the structures of prayer and contemplation will have been put in place and, through the steady repetition of the past 40 days, will have become a habit, part of the fabric of your daily lives.

But my prayer also is that every one of us looks beyond the confines of our own story to engage with the stories of those around us, seeking and finding biblical truths within each one, telling and retelling the wonderful story of Christ's saving action.

As we continue beyond Easter, we look for the promises of Pentecost and take upon ourselves the great commission as we continue to share all that the life, death and resurrection of Christ means for us and for the world.

My prayers are for you as your story continues.

Some final reflections

- What have I learned about myself during this Lenten period?
- What have I learned about God?
- How might I sustain a practice of prayer and reflection?
- How might I share all that God means to me – and all that he could mean to others?

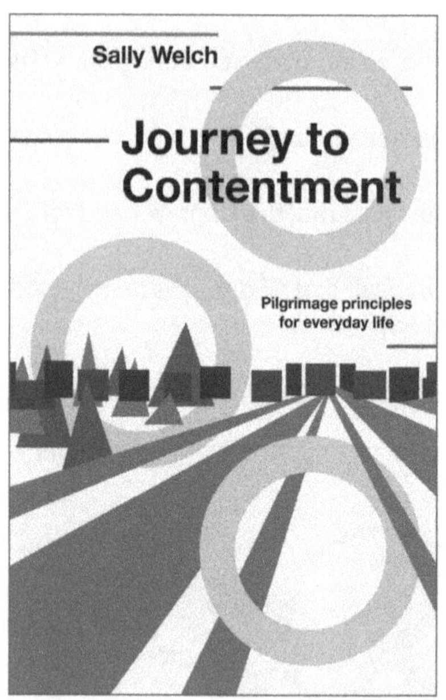
Sally Welch
Journey to Contentment
Pilgrimage principles for everyday life

SALLY WELCH
PILGRIM JOURNEYS
Pilgrimage for walkers and armchair travellers